China: A History of China and East Asia

Ancient China, Imperial Dynasties, Communism, Capitalism, Culture, Martial Arts, Medicine, Military, People including Mao Zedong, Confucius, and Sun Tzu

Table of Contents

Chapter 4: A History Of Martial Arts In Ancient China..39

Chapter 5: Old World Medicine In Ancient China.........51

Introduction

I want to thank you and congratulate you for downloading the book, China: A History of China and East Asia.

This book contains everything you need to know about China's rich and exciting history.

China; from the look of it on the outside, it is clear that the world's most populous nation and one of the world's biggest economies didn't just start a few years ago. On the contrary, China, even if its landscape has changed over the years, is probably one of the oldest recorded civilizations. With a vast landscape, world wonders, its rich diversified culture, its politics, social and economic might, you can bet that China, as it is, has a long story to tell. Think about it; China boasts of great prowess in martial arts like Kung Fu, its philosophies like Confucius, religion, the Chinese language, its alternative treatment breakthroughs like acupuncture and herbal treatments, great wonders like the Great Wall of China along with its rich recorded history dating back to as early as over 3000 years ago. That's not all; China boasts of a unique dynastic history, great military innovation, medicinal breakthroughs, and some of the most legendary figures the world has ever seen. You probably cannot find that in many other parts of the world.

So how did all these things come into being? How did The People's Republic of China become what it is today? Well, this book seeks to reveal to you just that. It includes lots of vital information that will enable you to have a good understanding of how the country was shaped into what it is today. As you will discover, China's history is as storied as a Walt Disney film that has everything. This book will give you comprehensive knowledge of China's sizable history.

Thanks again for downloading this book, I hope you enjoy it! If you do enjoy it, can you please leave a review on Amazon? I would greatly appreciate it.

P.S. You can email me anytime at
adambrownauthor@gmail.com
and let me know what you think. I am open to suggestions and will improve this book.

Chapter 1:
Ancient Chinese Dynasties

What is a Dynasty?

Dynasty means a series of rulers from the same family. Historical periods in China have the name of the family that dominated the country during that time. Some dynasties lasted for many centuries.

1: Xia Dynasty

About 2000 BC the occupants of what is now Northern China, near the Yellow River, came under the rule of the Xia Dynasty. There is no evidence for this dynasty, apart from some records compiled much later by reliable historians. It is believed that in this dynasty the use of bronze began. Bronze casting seems to have occurred at Erlitou during the Xia dynasty.

2: Shang Dynasty

The dynasty that followed the Xia dynasty was the Shang dynasty. Like the Xia dynasty the existence of it was questioned. However during the 1920s archaeological excavations unearthed incontrovertible evidence of it. The Shang dynasty achieved much more than the Xia dynasty. During the Shang dynasty cities like Anyang and Zhengzhou were constructed.

At its height the Shang state only controlled a relatively small area of northern China, however it was a model for other rival States, such as the Zhou. The Shang system, under which society was organized was a form of feudalism, in which relatives of the king and other lords got land in return for service and loyalty.

Bronze manufacture and use continued during this dynasty. It is amazing that such a complicated process as the making then casting of bronze occurred so early in history. For brass to be made there have to be supplies of copper, tin, and lead.

There have to be miners for these different metals. There have to be supplies of fuel for the furnaces, which smelted these metals into bronze. Most bronze was used for ornaments and for ritual objects. Only a small amount was used as weaponry, very little was used in agriculture.

The last Shang king has been accused of drunkenness, incest, cannibalism, pornography and sadism among other things. The virtues that had once led to the elevation of the Shang had left them and so had their right to rule.

Dynasties, like seasons and planets, obey a pattern of cycles. They ascend and decline at the behest of Heaven. The Shang were doomed because Heaven had transferred its earthly mandate to a more virtuous line. The Shang were defeated by the Zhou, from the East, at the battle of Muye. It was inevitable that they would be defeated. Their place in history was over.

3: The Zhou Dynasty

Third and last of the pre-imperial dynasties was the Zhou dynasty. They replaced the Shang as supreme power along the Yellow River basin at a time of about 1045 BC. As is so often the case in Chinese history it is believed they had won the approval of Heaven by their outstanding virtue while Shang by their degeneracy had forfeited it. The Zhou was the third and the last of three Pre-Imperial dynasties. There would be nearly 800 years of Zhou rule in China.

In the course of the Zhou dynasty, there were some 39 kings who followed one another, mostly in an orderly father to son succession. None of the subsequent dynasties of China would last more than half as long. The Zhou dynasty probably has the world record for longevity of a dynasty.

The Zhou dynasties began well with a successful defense of the country against barbarians in the West. However, as the centuries passed the country became disunited and there was a lot of internal strife. Despite this, there were major steps in the organization of society in the realms of technology, construction, trade, and agriculture.

During this dynasty, some very important features of Chinese thought and philosophy came to the fore such as Confucianism and the Dao religion.

In the three pre-Imperial dynasties the ruler was a king. The king was a leader and a warrior and also a kind of Pope. He was an intermediary to heaven. Every week by means of a ritual he would consult his ancestors.

This was done in a fascinating way. Relics called *Oracle bones* were heated up and the cracks that formed on these bones were interpreted as answers to questions about the future. Questions inscribed on these bones are among the earliest examples of writing.

4: The Qin Dynasty

By the end of the fourth century BC, the Quin took over the ruling of China and retook the territory lost during the last part of the Zhou dynasties from the barbarians. The philosophy of Confucianism was abandoned and replaced with Legalism, which led to a great strengthening and centralization of the state.

In 240 BC a man called Zheng came to power and really advanced China as a state. He proclaimed himself Emperor. A title that all future dynasties would embrace. Zheng was a ruthless man suffering from paranoia and with a very cruel side, in much the same way as a number of twentieth-century dictators. It was during his reign that the Great Wall of China was built.

His tomb featured the famous Terracotta Army of thousands of life-size warriors who presumably to fight for the Emperor in the afterlife. Zheng had been an unpopular ruler due to the severity of his reign and when he died the Qin dynasty came to an end soon afterward as the result of an intrigue featuring the actions of Zheng's closest Li Si and a prominent eunuch called Zhao Gao

5: The Han Dynasty
In the place of the Qin dynasty came the Han Dynasty led by its first Emperor Gaozu in 206 BC. Gaozu had come from the lower classes in society and was initially very anti-intellectual. However, he realized the error of his ways when he heard some words of wisdom from his beautiful chamberlain. She was called Lu Jia and bore Gaozu a son.

The emperor took careful notice of the warning and began to place greater faith in the abilities of the intelligentsia. The Han came to be seen as a good dynasty, ruling over a peaceful, wealthy, far-flung empire. However, its future seemed a bit shaky in its earlier years.

Gaozu gave land and possessions to his relatives and supporters. This re-created the feudal system of the Zhou era, which was only slowly disestablished by subsequent Han emperors.

A very serious weakness was the natural instability that was always around when emperors fathered sons by a number of women. During Gaozu's final years a bitter struggle, behind the scenes, took place between Lu Jia who had given birth to the oldest son of Gaozu and the rising favorite Qi who had hopes that the succession would go to her own child. Qi's son was the Emperor's preferred but when he died in 195 BC the succession went to the son of Lu.

She was now the Empress dowager and was able to take a cruel revenge on Qi and rule China. When her young son died she installed a boy as emperor, and when he grew up enough to become a nuisance, she had him dispatched and replaced.

She tried to guarantee her relatives an unchallengeable position by removing noble families with bloody purges, giving their estates to her own relatives. Lu remained in power until her death in 180 BC her hopes for the future went wrong. In the struggle that followed her death the family of the Empress dowager was annihilated.

The Han dynasty now went through a time of consolidation with China expanding South, even venturing into Vietnam and Korea. The severities of the Qin legal code were steadily reduced so as to make the new status quo popular among the people.

The Han dynasty lasted for over 400 years, interrupted only once by the brief rebellion and coup of Wang Mang. The dynasty witnessed long periods of prosperity, and was notable for advances in the manufacture of iron, hydraulics, the making of paper and international trade.

Its influence was great as forever afterward the Chinese regarded a unified empire as normal even when periods of disunity lasted for hundreds of years. From that time on they referred to themselves as the 'Sons of Han' and in many respects they regarded the Han empire is the model for the future.

The fall of the Han, like the fall of the Roman empire, was followed by a long period of local struggles that might be described as being similar to the Dark Ages in the West. There was a total of six dynasties during this period of Chinese history.

6: The Six Dynasties

The six dynasties period of China ran from the end of the Han dynasty in 220 A.D. until the rise of the Sui dynasty in 589 A.D. The dynasties were:

Wu 222-280, Dong Jin 317 - 420, Liu-Song 420 - 479 Nin Qi 479 - 502 Nan Liang 502-557 Nan Chen 557-589.

The period in which these men ruled featured struggles between landowners and peasants, the military and the large number of non-ethnic Chinese who had been settled in the North, officials and local rulers.

When the Han disappeared China was divided into 3 Kingdoms Wei in the North, Shu in the Southwest, and Wu in the South. During this time of turmoil various regimes came and went.

At any time during the 6 dynasties, there was never one Emperor to rule a united China. During the period 317-420, which features Dong Jin, there was a part of China, which was called the 16 Kingdoms. These were not under Dong's control.

The Chinese have long been fascinated by the personalities, conflicts, and feats of arms of this period. There are famous literary works relating to all of this.

The 6 Dynasties were an age of appalling violence and bloodshed, not very different from the last 400 years of European history. However, this period also witnessed a flowering of Chinese literature and arts and some radical cultural changes.

The most significant of all of these was the spread of Buddhism. This Indian religion became an integral part of the Chinese way of life, in which Confucianism, Daoism, and Buddhist values complement rather than struggle to overcome each other.

7: The Sui Dynasty

The Sui dynasty lasted from 581-618AD. There were only 2 Sui emperors. The Sui Dynasty began with the replacement of a Northern Zhou local ruler called Yuwen Pin by the Duke of Sui, a man of mixed ethnicity. He took the name Sui Wengdin when he became Emperor. Wengdin was a brutal man but he reunited China with some highly planned, brilliantly executed military campaigns.

During his rule the Buddhist religion flourished. Nearly 4000 temples and pagodas were built during this time. Proscriptions against both Buddhism and Daoism were abolished.

He was succeeded by his youngest son who became Sui Yangdin The emperor Yangdin was cruel and violent. His reign was marked by some great feats including the building of canals, albeit at great human cost.

In order to become ruler, he intrigued against his older brother, killed his father and raped some of the wives of his father, according to Chinese historians. One of the things that contributed to the fall of the dynasty was a series of disastrous military campaigns against the Koreans.

8: The Tang Dynasty

After the Sui dynasty, there was a dynasty of 300 years. This was the Tang dynasty. The first ruler of this dynasty was a man called Li Yuan. He overthrew Sui Yangdin who had fled self following a military defeat. Li Yuan called himself Tang Gaozu after proclaiming himself as Emperor.

The second Tang ruler was his son, Tang Taizong. Taizong was a brilliant emperor. He was particularly sensible at taking good advice from his ministers. The minister who he was dependent upon most was called Wei Zheng. This man was almost a saint and had the highest principles.

The third Tang ruler was Tang Gaozong. He was married to the Empress Wu. When he passed away she intrigued to become the only sovereign in Chinese history that was a woman.

Empress Wu was very sexy, indeed promiscuous, but very able despite being recorded in a most unfavorable way by the historians of ancient China. Confucianism regarded woman as second class citizens who should never lead the Empire.

The century 650 - 750 AD, was a wonderful one for China and could be called the first Chinese century. It was a period when the Chinese empire was completely restored, there was much trade with other countries such as India, Persia, Vietnam, Korea and Japan.

The apex of the Tang period was in the rain of Tang Xuanzong who reigned from 712 - 756 AD. Buddhism continued to flourish in the Tang period. Indeed its influence grew. During the Tang Dynasty, the capital city alternated between Chang'an and Luo Yang.

The Tang dynasty saw the Chinese Empire taken to limits it had not reached before, nor ever again. It was believed that the safeguarding of the borders of the Empire was a task best suited to non-Han peoples and it was this policy, which paved the way for the disasters, which soon came.

A man called An Lushan of non-Chinese pedigree intrigued his way into Imperial favor, particularly that of one of the Emperor's mistresses a very beautiful woman called Yang Guifei. When he and she had an affair the emperor found out and An Lushan had to flee the capital.

He raised an army and fought a campaign, which eventually saw him sack the capital Chang'an. As this happened the emperor fled along with his mistress Yang Giifei and his chief Minister Yang Guozhong.

During this flight, both the Yangs were killed. The emperor eventually abdicated in favor of his son Tan Suzong. Over a period of years, the Tangs regained their capital Chang'an and the core of the empire but their high tide had passed.

In the late ninth century, a man called Huang Chao led a campaign against the Tangs, which finished with his army capturing then sacking Chang'an. The Tang Dynasty was virtually finished. The Tangs were followed by a short period called the Five Dynasties.

9: Five Dynasties

This was a very short period in the long history of China. It covered the years 907-960 A.D. This was a period of much disorder during which China splintered into 10 kingdoms with a total of 40 different rulers. Although disastrous politically for the Empire this era saw the establishment in China of two things, which are of great importance in our modern world.

The first of these was the printing press with movable type. A bureaucrat called Feng Dao made a major use of this. In addition to this, he was also frugal, generous and decent. In the eyes of his biographers his loyal service to five different dynasties was a disgrace and an insult to all that the biographers believed in so he was not given a very good write up.

Another innovation, which was of crucial importance, both now and then, was paper money. As a consequence in some of the kingdoms, there was a boom in trade and commerce.

During this period the capital was located back to Luo Yang but was sometimes moved to Kaifeng. Chang'an the old capital was still in ruins.

10: The Song dynasty

This dynasty ruled during the period 960- 1297 AD. The first Song emperor was Taizu who came to power after long periods in which he gained the support of his generals. He died in 976 AD.

During the Song dynasty, there was a great flowering of arts in China and an expansion of the Confucian exams for the official class. The anti-martial ethos of Confucianism came to dominate China and during the period of the Song dynasty, the power of the military became much less.

During the reign of the first two emperors the empire was enlarged again but then things stabilized. Initially, the Song dynasty was in the North, centered in Kaifeng, and was known as the Northern Song. After a defeat by the Jin, the center of the empire moved to Lin'an in South China from Kaifeng in North China.

In 1235 the Song made an incredible blunder by attacking the Mongols who were the greatest military power in the world. The Mongols were initially diverted elsewhere but eventually attacked China and in doing so brought the Song dynasty to an end.

11: The Yuan Dynasty

Kublai Khan became ruler of China in 1271 AD and Emperor in 1279 AD. His name as emperor was Shizu of Yuan. He had founded the first and only non-Chinese dynasty, the Yuan dynasty.

He moved the capital of China to Beijing, which was not too far from Mongolia. He went to great lengths to ensure his troops did not become soft by being stationed in China.

The Chinese were forced to pay an extra tax in order that the occupation was paid for. Mongol rule was not popular in China. The Yuan dynasty ended in 1368.

12: The Ming Dynasty

In 1368 Hongwu became the first Chinese emperor after the Yuan dynasty had fallen. He was the first emperor of the Ming Dynasty. This dynasty lasted from 1368 - 1644 AD. Hongwu was a bloodthirsty man who did not like the mandarins. He killed thousands of them. From his reign onwards their power was greatly reduced.

Hongwu's son Yongle was the third Ming emperor. He was a brilliant soldier and expanded the empire. During the reign of Yongle huge junks filled with thousands of soldiers made long trips to all points of the Indian Ocean, perhaps to Australia, and even to America. Unfortunately, all seaborne expeditions ceased after the death of Yongle.

In 1517 A.D. the Portuguese arrived and everything began to change although the Mings did not realize how important this event was. More and more Europeans arrived. They only traded initially and there was no threat from them yet.

The quality of emperors declined and in 1644 f the last Ming emperor hung himself on a hill over Beijing as a rebel leader entered the city.

13: The Qing Dynasty

This dynasty was the last Imperial dynasty in China. It ruled in the period 1644-1911. The Qing dynasty was a foreign one as the Qings were Manchus. Unlike the Mongols of many centuries earlier they had adopted Chinese customs and are regarded as Chinese.

Under them, the empire expanded to what it is today. In 1689 the Qings defeated the Russians in the siege of Albazin. Unfortunately for the Qings, the inevitable decline in the quality of their emperors was occurring when a foe of unimaginable power appeared in the form of the British. By selling opium in large amounts to the Chinese the British bankrupted China then fought a war against them, which the British easily won.

As a consequence, they got concessions in China. Following their success the Americans and the French also got concessions. An Empress Cixi came to power and allied herself with some rebels called the Boxers. They declared war on the foreigners but were beaten. China had also been beaten by Japan in a war just before that. China was in a bad way.

The Empress died in 1908 and the dynasty ended in 1911. This brought to an end the dynasties of China. A new world was born.

Chapter 2:
Communism, Capitalism And Its Role In Shaping China & East Asia

China

During October 1911 a revolution took place in southern China, which led to the end of the Qing dynasty. As a result of the revolution, the Republic of China was formed. The leader of this revolution was Sun Yat Sen.

As is always the case in revolutions there was chaos with a period from 1916 to 1925 of warlord rule in many places. Throughout China, there were deep resentments of foreign countries. China had been attacked and humiliated by them repeatedly in the 19th century. The foreign powers still had concessions in Shanghai and other places in China. This was abhorrent to nearly all Chinese no matter whether they were rich or poor.

Sun Yat Sen had appealed to Britain, and to America for recognition of his wished-for democratic regime at Canton, and assistance to overthrow the ruinous rule of the warlords. His appeal was rejected. In rejecting this error of monumental proportions was made for reasons that today are seen as being naive and very shortsighted.

The warlords were weak and corrupt. They didn't care for China's best interests; only their own. They loved the concessions that gave them a bolt hole when things went against them. They were able to invest their ill-gotten gains safely, under the shield of the foreigner's law. They could stay there, plotting and scheming, safe from being arrested.

The inspiration for the Chinese Revolution in 1911 had been western and democratic. However, it wasn't recognized as such by the West and an extraordinary historical opportunity missed. As a consequence, the Chinese revolutionaries themselves rejected it.

They turned to Communism, as a result of Russian help, encouragement, fair and equal treatment. In 1921 Sun Yet-sen met Joffe, a Russian envoy, in Shanghai. There was an agreement that declared that both parties had come to the recognition that Communism was not right for China. Sun accepted on behalf of the Kuomintang or Nationalist Party (this was the new name), Russian aid and alliance with the new Chinese Communist Party.

The Kuomintang became just like the Russian Communist party. It had political commissars, mass propaganda outlets, and very strict discipline, It did not work for a democratic republic the goal was now for a party dictatorship which would run the country for several years until the people were able to govern themselves.

The Chinese Communist party was founded in 1921. Among the founders was Mao Tse-tung, then a library assistant in Ch¹en's university, and, among a group of students in Paris, Chou En-lai. Mao was a middle peasant or yeoman in origin, the son of a farmer who was a land owner, employed laborers, and was able to read and have an education for his son. Chou came from a wealthy mandarin background.

None of these early foundation members and later leaders had seen Communism in Russia or understood the Russian language. This had extremely important ramifications later on as the decades passed.

After the death of Sun in 1925 the Kuomintang, based in Canton prepared for an expedition to conquer the north and destroy the warlords. Genuine reform, an army of a good standard and revolutionary zeal were marks of the new rulers in Canton.

Foreigners were certain that the Kuomintang would never defeat the more martial northerners. This expedition started, under the leadership of Chiang Kai-shek, early in 1926. Chiang Kai-shek had been sent for special training in Moscow by Sun Yat-sen and on his return had set up and commanded the new military training college at Whampoa. This college produced the best-known generals of the Kuomintang and also the future leading generals of the Communist army.

The expedition was victorious. Warlords were overcome one by one and the soldiers of the expedition were closing in on Shanghai. As the expedition proceeded so did social revolution. The Communist organizers spread through the rural areas inciting the peasants against their landlords, while others agitated among the workers of Shanghai, who loathed their poverty and exploitation.

At the news of the coming army the Shanghai workers, under the Communist leadership of Chou En-Lai took over the Chinese part of the city from the warlord's troops. When the Nationalist armies arrived all opposition surrendered and the foreigners confronted the forces of the revolution.

Chiang Kai-shek had known for a long time that his alliance with Communist revolution could not last. It had been useful so far but the days of such utility were gone. He was in danger of losing his position of leadership. The Nationalist government was now in Wu Han. It had moved from Canton, which was very left wing, under the influence or Russian advisers.

These advisers were actually insisting the Communists keep along with the Kuomintang. Stalin's instructions were that the Communist party was unable to carry out a revolution alone but must help the Kuomintang carry one out. Chiang struck and executed those Communist leaders he could catch. Among those Communist leaders in Shanghai who escaped, was Chou En-Lai.

Chiang separated from the Wu Han government to set up his own right-wing Nationalist government based in Nanking. This break with the Communist party was the beginning of the Chinese revolution that saw the Communists victorious in 1949.

During this time the Japanese were conquering large areas of China but rather than do something about them Chiang devoted his time and energy in campaigns to try and destroy the Communists. The Communists could not be suppressed. Chiang persisted in this folly for ten years.

Mao and his colleagues established a new kind of Communist regime. Its main interest was the peasants, with land reform as its focus, warfare using guerilla tactics for defense, avoiding the cities, inciting the peasants as its political aim.

This was absolute heresy to Russian and conventional Marxist teaching. Mao was expelled from the Central Political Committee, of the official party. Some say he was purged from this party. No one knows.

For years Mao's Communists were cut off from all ways of communicating with the outside world and were unable to get the orders from Moscow. They had to do their own thinking. If they had followed the orders of Moscow they would have been totally unsuccessful.

Initially, the method of appealing to the peasants' hunger for land was viciously applied. They encouraged peasants to kill landlords, often cruelly. Officials of the Kuomintang were executed, non-supporters or opponents received harsh treatment. The Communists went out of their way to be the friend of the peasant. Wreaking violence upon the traditional enemies of the peasant seemed the best way to do this.

In order to avoid Chiang, the Communists mimicked the long march of Huang Chao in the ninth century and walked to Yenan where they lived in caves and carried out their revolution. It was from there that they launched the campaigns that saw them become rulers of China.

The Kuomintang could have prevented this. The Kuomintang was the prisoner of the ancient Chinese social system. It tried to alter the direction of the revolution, to bring stability to society while clinging to the past. As well as a reactionary looking back the Kuomintang failed because of selfishness, greed, and nepotism. An age was ending and the Kuomintang did not have what was required to usher in the new age.

In 1936 it was clear that a crisis was approaching. The Communists had completed their Long March, they were plainly not going away. In December 1936, Chiang Kai-shek was planning one more 'extermination drive' against the Communists in Xi'an. Unbeknownst to him the whole world was about to change.

The army facing the Communists there consisted of local Shensi forces and the North-Eastern Army of Chiang. To make a long story short Chiang was captured and under threat of his life went into an agreement with the Communists to fight the Japanese. This agreement lasted reasonably well until the Japanese were beaten. Once they were the gloves came off!

At the end of the war Chiang Kai-shek got the U.S. Air Force to transport his troops to the areas occupied by the Communists and thus obtain the surrender or the Japanese to the Kuomintang, not to the Communists. In addition, the Japanese were ordered to defend all ground they held against Communist attack and surrender only to Kuomintang forces.

So it was that their Japanese occupiers to Nationalist forces flown in by the U.S.A.F surrendered cities in areas where Communist guerrillas were in control, and where Kuomintang had not been in evidence for eight years. This was absolutely unacceptable to the Communists. It did not endear the Americans to them.

The Russians betrayed them in a different way. The Russians had occupied Manchuria near the end of the Second World War and could have handed this developed region in China, to the Chinese Communists outright. Instead, they handed the cities to the Kuomintang but let the Communists take over the countryside. They also stole all the plant from the factories!

Despite these betrayals, the Communists won the civil war, which raged until 1949. At its end, Mao ascended the Gates of Heavenly Peace and proclaimed, "This country will never again be insulted by foreigners. We have stood up"

Initially, there was a period of calm in China after the chaos of the Civil War then land reforms began. Shortly after they had begun, in October 1950, China became involved in the Korean War. 3 million Chinese soldiers served in that war and about 200,000 were killed in it. Mao lost his oldest son, Mao AnYing, in that conflict.

Mao was very keen to get an atomic bomb and after the Korean War, he began requisitioning grain from the peasants. This caused great hardship and was made much worse in 1955 when the peasants were forced to live in collective farms. At the same time, he nationalized all industry and commerce.

In 1956 an event occurred that triggered the eventual break between Russia and China. Khrushchev, the new leader of Russia, denounced Stalin for his fiendish behavior and murder of millions of innocent people. As well Mao did not get the atomic weapons from Russia that he desperately wanted.

In 1957 Mao said, "Let 100 flowers bloom," which means he was letting people speak their minds. As they did so if they were critical of his policies they were arrested, humiliated and tortured.

After that in 1958, he launched the Great Leap Forward, which was his plan to create the industry that would produce enough material so that he could win a big war. The Great Leap Forward was an appalling disaster, which caused the death of tens of millions as a result of starvation.

In 1959 Mao ordered his army to invade Tibet, which he claimed had always been a part of China. In 1960 the split between Khrushchev and Mao became public after Mao publicly stated that a nuclear war would be perfectly all right if it was succeeded by a communist world. The Russians strongly disagreed and removed their advisers from China.

In 1962 Mao started a brief and indecisive war with India. In 1964 the Chinese finally tested their first nuclear weapon at Lop Nor in a remote part of China.

Throughout his reign, Mao was an iconoclast who destroyed many of the architectural and artistic treasures of the Chinese past. He also deprived the people of entertainment. People were force-fed propaganda and there was a personality cult of Mao that was very similar to that which now exists in North Korea.

In 1966 the Cultural Revolution began. This was also a disaster and millions of people were killed. In 1969 there was a small war with Russia. The Russians sounded out the Americans about a joint strike on the nuclear facilities of the Chinese. This was refused and led to the extraordinary events of the next four decades.

In 1972 there was a rapprochement between the USA and China. President Richard Nixon had talks with Mao and in so doing started a process that is still proceeding. Mao died in 1976 of Lou Gehrig's disease, a pathetic old man racked with regret and paranoia.

Deng Xiaoping came to power in 1978 and initiated great changes. He freed many able and innocent people who had been persecuted and imprisoned. However for tactical reasons, probably based on history, he did not repudiate Mao.

He started the one child policy. He began to trade with all countries. The greatest transformation of any country in history took place. An impoverished country imprisoned with Stalinist communism was completely changed.

Its rulers embraced capitalism in all ways except the name *capitalism*. The Communist Party is communist by name only. Its main function is to control the population. The Revolution has come full circle, history in China has been repeated once more. The old order fell, a period of chaos after its collapse, then from within Chinese history and tradition a new order has emerged.

With the USA abandoning its allies and repudiating its policies against global warming and free trade. China has an opportunity to promote its way of doing things to the whole world. In January 2017 the leader of China attended a meeting of the world's best and most powerful economic leaders and declared Chinese support for free trade.

China already has created the best solar industry in the world. If they can find ways of successfully stopping global warming and ways of expanding free trade then most countries will use them and China will rule the world.

East Asia, Asia, Pacific

In the 15th century Vasco da Gama, a Portuguese explorer, rounded the Cape of Good Hope and reached Asia. So began centuries of interaction between Europe and the countries of the Asian continent.

Initially, the European countries only came to trade but later they conquered many of these countries and set up colonies. This process of the colonization of Asia by Europeans was largely complete by the end of the 19th century.

During the 19th century Japan, in the North Pacific, had become a major industrial power. It built a huge fleet and beat the Russians very badly in a war at the beginning of the 20th century. It wanted an empire so it attacked, conquered and colonized Korea in 1910. It wanted more and attacked China after the First World War.

When France was totally defeated by the Nazis in 1940 Japan took over Vietnam. The Japanese attacked America and Britain in 1941 but by attacking the United States made a very bad mistake and was defeated in a ferocious three and a half year war, which resulted in millions of casualties.

At the end of the Second World War, all of Asia had been convulsed. The European powers were all exhausted by the demands of that war. The old way in Asia with these bankrupt and broken countries running things was finished.

The first of these European countries to realize this was Britain that soon released India and Pakistan as independent countries in 1947. There were other British colonies in Asia but they avoided the horrors that befell the colonies of other European countries.

Holland in the past had controlled the Dutch East Indies yet it had been defeated by the Nazi onslaught early in 1940. At the end of the war, it tried to reassert its authority in these Indies. It failed and they became Indonesia.

Indonesia

Indonesia used to be the Dutch East Indies. It has been an independent country since 1949. Its first president was a man called Sukarno. It nearly became communist in 1965, however, a coup saw this suppressed and a new leader called Suharto came to power.

Mao advised the Communists in Indonesia to have a revolution. It failed badly and led to millions of deaths and a ban on communism. Indonesia is the largest Muslim country in the world and has many resources. It is now a democracy and has a population of about 260 million people. There are nearly three million Chinese people in Indonesia.

Indochina

France had been in control of Indochina, which was the group of countries: Cambodia, Laos, and Vietnam. After the Second World War, the French tried to reassert their colonial control. Their attempts came to an end in 1954 at the battle of Den Bien Phu when the Vietnamese rebels led by Ho Chi Minh defeated the French very badly. As a consequence, France left Indochina and those countries became independent.

Unfortunately, Vietnam was divided. North Vietnam was a communist country led by Ho Chi Minh. South Vietnam was a very unstable country much like China had been before the Communists took over. It was the desire of Ho Chi Minh to unite both parts of Vietnam into one country.

The United States had led a coalition of nations that successfully prevented a takeover of the entire Korean peninsula by communists earlier in the 1950s and was anxious that there was no communist takeover of South Vietnam.

From 1954 until 1972 the US unsuccessfully waged a war, with the help of a number of allies, against the South Vietnamese rebels, the Vietcong, and North Vietnam to prevent a communist takeover. During this war, they dropped three times the tonnage of bombs that were dropped by all the warring countries during World War II. The Americans left Indochina in 1975.

Initially, Cambodia, Laos, and a reunited Vietnam were communist countries but like China, they seem to have abandoned communism and embraced capitalism. Vietnam is similar to China in that it retained its Communist Party as a government.

All of South East Asia is rich in resources. Although trade is done with all countries the country with which they most trade is China. China is the country that will eventually have the most influence in South East Asia.

India

Although not regarded as part of East Asia India is a huge Asian country with strong links to both China and the rest of Asia. India was never a communist country however India had a very socialist economy, until late in the 20th century, which was very inefficient.

Although it has not transformed itself as much as China it is certainly making great progress and is a major world power with a huge population and vast resources. India fought a brief war with China in 1962. There have been few problems since then, however, the border between these two great countries is a source of potential conflict.

Australia and New Zealand

These countries are not really Asian but what happens to China and the rest of Asia is very important to them and what they do is very important to Asia.

Australia is a vast country with abundant resources. Until recently trade with China in these resources was growing enormously. This has now slowed right down.

New Zealand is a much smaller country but one which is closely aligned to Australia. Both these countries have been deeply affected by the way of the United States is abandoning free-trade and are looking for free-trade agreements with China and other Asian countries.

Chapter 3:
Ancient Chinese Culture

Yin and Yang

This is a concept, which is largely foreign in the West but is one that is absolutely central to a comprehension of all parts of the life of the Chinese people. This applies from ancient times until the 21st century.

Basically the idea of Yin Yang is that everything has two halves, which can and should be in perfect balance but usually they are not as the two halves are always dynamically transforming one into the other. While this transformation is occurring the whole is maintained.

Examples are Female (Yin), Male (Yang) or Cold (Yin) Heat (Yang). Yin and Yang are usually associated with another important principle and that is the Principle of 5 Elements or 5 Phases.

The concept of Yin Yang runs throughout, and can be seen in, every part of Chinese Culture.

History Of Confucianism: The Life Of Confucius

Confucius was China's greatest philosopher. He lived 551-479 BC during the Spring and Autumn periods of the Zhou Dynasty. Little is known about the life of Confucius. He was born in the small state of Lu and probably belongs to the class of gentry that was becoming impoverished during this period. Consequently, he was seeking paid official posts.

Confucius himself does not seem to have risen very high in the service of Lu, and when, in old age, he visited other courts in order to give rulers the benefits of his incisive thought, he found none willing to employee him. Like many prophets, he was a failure in his own time. However, his teachings were transmitted orally through his disciples and his words were recorded in the volume known as the *Analects*.

Seeing himself as one who wished to restore the past rather than innovate, Confucius advocated the performance of all the traditional rituals. He had no interest in discussing gods, spirits or the afterlife, insisting that it was quite difficult enough to solve problems on the human level without venturing into the spiritual world. Many later Confucian scholars followed the philosopher's example.

Confucius approved of such practices because they were socially useful, and none more so than ancestor worship, which extended into the afterlife the hierarchical principles of filial piety on which the family was organized. Such hierarchies, with fixed roles and relationships, were what held society together.

Each person must perform his or her part and one of his most famous sayings was," Let the ruler rule, the minister administer, the father be a father, the son be a son." This would have been a dreadful endorsement of existing authority if Confucius had not also insisted that in each role a person must behave dutifully and benevolently. Only then can harmony prevail.

Language

The Chinese alphabet is unique. Instead of a few dozen letters, it has thousands of characters. It is not really like the similar alphabets of Korea and Japan. In spite of its complexity, it usefully serves a population of hundreds of millions of people. Most of the Chinese population is literate and are quite able to read a newspaper. For someone to read a Chinese newspaper paper with understanding you would need to know a minimum of 2000- 3000 characters.

The first Chinese writing dates from 3500 BC although some say it is much older. The writing made its first appearance during the Shang dynasty on what are called *Oracle Bones*. Objects used to divine the future made from the bones of animals. Initially, the writing depicted naturally occurring objects however that changed as the centuries passed and the scripts developed and became more stylized and elegant.

Later examples of the written Chinese language are found on old decorations and sculptures. Seven scripts can be identified in the development of the modern written language. The most recent development occurred in 1949 when a more simplified form was brought into Communist China to replace the traditional characters called Kaishu.

Of the Chinese countries, the People's Republic and Singapore use the simplified script but other Chinese countries like Taiwan and Hong Kong have opted to continue to use the traditional script.

The population of China is about 1.3 billion and it covers a vast area. 70% of the population speaks Mandarin with other major dialects being spoken. Two of the dialects are Cantonese and

Min. Although Chinese may not be able to understand each other's dialect they can all understand the same written language. In this respect the written language is a source of unity.

Spirituality & Religion

For hundreds of years, writers on Chinese religion have talked about the three-ways, which are Confucianism, Daoism, and Buddhism. These three religions have shaped the way that people in China think about life, death, and the heavens for more than 2000 years. Confucianism and Daoism are homegrown religions that originated in China itself. Buddhism came to China from India about 2000 years ago.

For much of China's history, the three religions have existed peacefully side-by-side. Many Chinese people who practice worship have not felt the need to choose one religion and reject the others. People take those parts of these religions based on what is most suited to them from any of the three.

From the philosophy of Confucius, they have learned the importance of a code of ethics based on respect for others and the maintaining of the correct relationships between father and child, husband and wife, ruler and ruled.

In this respect, Confucianism was also an important tool for maintaining the power of the Chinese royal family in Imperial times. Emperors worshiped heaven and believed that this gave them their mandate to rule, but they employed Confucian scholars to run their civil service.

In Daoism, the Chinese have found a very different philosophy, one that seeks to follow a way, the Dao, which involves sensitivity to the patterns of the universe, and the nurturing of the natural flow of energy through the body.

Buddhism brought a way of understanding the suffering in the world and a way of leaving it behind. The Chinese adopted Buddhism with its many deities and some schools of Chinese Buddhism are based on devotion to these saintly beings.

All of the three ways have been combined and developed in Chinese popular religion, in which people seek the help of the gods, Daoist immortals or deified figures such as Confucius.

Literature

Some Neolithic poetry found in China carries designs that may or may not be written characters. But the earliest certain examples of a script, recognizably the ancestor of the modern Chinese language, are the questions and answers scratched onto Oracle Bones late in the Shang period.

Its association with religious ritual may be a reason why the written word came to be regarded with such reverence, and why those who possessed the ability to write obtained recognition as a cultural and political elite. Reverence for writing also inevitably makes references to the attitudes and doctrines of the past, as perceived in books, and this perhaps explains the conservatism of traditional China, in which originality was not prized or praised, and change, when it did occur, was generally presented in terms of a reinterpretation or reworking of the existing heritage.

The literary heritage derives from the five Confucian classics, a collection of writings from the Zhou period. They were believed to have been edited or composed by Confucius himself. They comprised the *I Ching* which is called *The Book of Changes* which was used for divination; prescriptions for ritual and conduct; materials from which came the remarkable tradition of Chinese historical writing and *The Book of Songs*, the first known collection of Chinese poetry. *The Book of Songs* contains 305 poems, said to have been selected by Confucius himself and certainly used by him in his teaching.

Most of them probably date from the 9th to 7th century BC. Poetry was an ancient art and it was also one that became closely linked with the imperial system. Its prestige was such that the common people revered it and an emperor found nothing incongruous about reading his own verses aloud to encourage workers toiling on the canal system.

As early as the Han period literature was recognized as having a value independent of any moral or social message it might transmit, literary fame was seen as an antidote to the oblivion inflicted by death. Educated persons habitually quoted poetry to one another, a practice encouraged by the examination system that was used in Imperial China.

Music & Dancing Styles

Music was one of the essential elements in Chinese life, ranging from work songs to the hymns accompanying Confucian ceremonial. Inscriptions on Shang Oracle Bones demonstrates that flutes, drums, stone chimes and bells were already being played in that long-distant era.

Archaeological discoveries of the subsequent Zhou period included the use of all of these and also mouth organs, panpipes, and early versions of perhaps the most distinctive Chinese instrument the zither.
As in other cultures song and poetry were closely related and the early verses preserved in *The Book of Songs* may well have been selected by court musicians to make up a repertoire of

lyrical, ceremonial and martial pieces on which they could draw at need.

By Han times, wealthy families had musicians among their employees, their stances in performance preserved in tomb decorations.

Dance has also been important in China, having a long history. There are records of dancing in both the Zhou and Qin Dynasty periods. Dancing reached it's peak in the Tang Dynasty but suffered a decline in later dynasties.

Pictures of the early dancing show people dancing in a line and holding hands in such a way that it is clear they are performing some religious or ceremonial ritual. Later during the Zhou dynasty, there were six styles that record the Great Six Dances. These dances also had a religious significance.

Painting

Nothing is known of painting as an independent activity until the Han period. The art was already flourishing, as is made clear by references in literary sources to great cycles of wall paintings, which illustrated Confucian moral subjects or the rival Daoist world of myth and magic. Unfortunately, none of these objects have survived or if they did then they have not been found yet.

Our knowledge of Han painting, as of other Han arts, comes from the excavation of tombs, and with the exception of a splendid, mysterious, symbol-rich painted banner from the Han period, the works that have been recovered from them are decorations on brick walls, boxes, and similar objects.

These can hardly be representative of Han painting as a whole, yet they do display some characteristics of Chinese art that are found through much of its history, in particular, fluent, sensitive brush lines and superb use of color.

The century and a half following the collapse of the Han empire are virtually blank in the history of Chinese painting. Great art obviously flourished among the southern dynasties, but only one artist can be linked to a specific work.

As we go on further there is evidence of brilliant artwork. Unfortunately not as much of it has been preserved as we would like. The Chinese had a different way of showing perspective but they certainly able to use this.

Sculpture

The Chinese have excelled at carving on the small scale in a number of media, including jade and ivory as well as wood and stone. Their achievement in large-scale sculpture has been more limited and is mainly associated with the imagery and styles introduced by Buddhism, the Indian religion imported from that country.

Although some large-scale stone carving may have been practiced earlier, during the Shang period, the examples that survive are relatively small. Apart from fragments of relief carving, they consist of seated figures of people, tigers and other animals in marble or limestone. Solid, frontally posed and carved with minimal detail or articulation, they give an impression of monumentality despite their size. The complex designs engraved on their services are related to those found on contemporary bronzes and reinforce the impression of hieratic remoteness that they convey.

Some wooden ritual objects have been recovered from the kingdom of Chu, one of the leading warring states, whose conquest by Qin was the final step in the creation of the Chinese empire.

The most monumental objects associated with the First Emperor were not of stone or wood but the ceramic army of life-size men and horses that guarded his tomb. The monumental stone sculpture has survived from the Han dynasty in the form of figures of real and fantastic beasts lining the processional way to the tombs.

Some tomb walls were decorated with low reliefs, which were linear rather than sculptural in character. On the available evidence, there was nothing to suggest that Chinese sculpture would soon take a radical new direction.

The introduction of the Buddhist religion provided the spur for some marvelous works. There were some giant sculptures of Buddha made within cave complexes. As the vitality of Buddhism declined so did the stone carvings and the tradition associated with it,

Lacquer

Some works of arts can only be created with a substantial investment of labor and great technical skill. We should expect them to have been made from the beginning for the luxury market of a relatively advanced and sophisticated society. Surprisingly, this was far from the case with two celebrated and highly distinctive products of Chinese civilization which were objects of lacquer and objects of jade.

These were being fashioned as early as the Neolithic period for the Chinese had begun to make use of metals. The discovery of lacquer is certainly remarkable. The substance is the sap of the lacquer tree, which at that time grew in China and was obtained like rubber, by tapping.

After suitable treatment, it could be colored with pigments mostly red and black and used like a paint or varnish to coat woods, hemp cloth or other material. Its functional values lay in the fact that it was impervious to heat and it was waterproof, enabling it to be used to protect kitchenware and furniture.

But it was also decorative; it's shiny, colorful services giving distinction to boxes, caps, shoes, military equipment, coffins and many other items. Designs could be painted in lacquer onto the lacquer ground that covered an object.

By the Han era lacquer working was an important industrial art, and production line techniques prevailed in state factories, where different craftsmen carried out half a dozen or more specialist tasks. One cup, from that era, is actually inscribed with a list of the craftsmen involved.

Jade

Nothing was more precious to the Chinese than jade, which was endowed with seemingly magical qualities. Though not indestructible, it is so hard that even steel tools cannot be used to carve it. It is translucent, smooth and ice cold to the touch; it makes a musical note when struck, and takes an oily polish.

Despite their reverence for this mysterious material the Chinese discovered jade could be shaped by using quartzite or other abrasive powders in conjunction with rubbing or boring implements. The process by which the jade is shaped is very slow indeed.

Jade objects dating from about 3500 BC have been found in the far northeast and in spectacularly large numbers at a Neolithic site in the Yangtze Delta. In both cases, the high standard of execution suggests that they were preceded by a long working tradition. Among them were objects that would continue to be fashioned for thousands of years such as a flat ring with a circular central aperture and a rectangular section.

Jade is not a single type of stone but describes a family with similar properties. The kind most commonly used by the Chinese was nephrite. The Maori uses nephrite in New Zealand and other people throughout the world use it.

Architecture

The traditional architecture of China creates a delightfully exotic impression that makes it easy to overlook the fundamental simplicity of its layout and construction. Whether they were intended as modest houses or magnificent palaces, dwellings consisted of the rectangular hall like units, built almost entirely of wood.

They were constructed on the pillar and beam principle and a series of such pillars and beams provided the framework for the walls and the base for the roof structure, which consisted of a kingpost, rising from the center of each beam to supports the ridge line of the pitched roof, plus a complicated set of rafters, purlins, and brackets.

If the hall was to be not only long but broad, secondary or tertiary sets of pillars might have to be added further forward or back, underneath the slope of the roof. Pillars, doors, windows and other features were laid out according to the principle of symmetry so dear to the Chinese.

The plan of Chinese dwellings was straightforward. Each was built in the form of a courtyard, with a main hall in the north from which two smaller, symmetrical wings extended at right angles to the south. The long inner side of the hall faced the entrance.

All Chinese buildings were designs to face due south unless the site made some modifications unavoidable. The positive, yang quality of a southern orientation was such that the main gate of a city was always in that quarter, and if the city was an imperial capital a grand processional way led through the gate to the southern entrance of the palaces, the inner sanctum of the emperor being located at the furthest, northernmost point of the complex.

Similarly, a well-off family built their mansion in the form of a double court, the first allocated to domestic staff and visitors, while the northernmost court at the bank was reserved for the family.

The most imposing traditional buildings to have survived are those in the Forbidden City, the Imperial Palace complex in Beijing. Surrounded by a moat and a 14.4-mile wall, it was formerly parts of the world Imperial City which itself stood within the walled city proper. The Forbidden City was constructed for the Ming emperor in 1404 AD.

Chapter 4:
A History Of Martial Arts In Ancient China

For many Westerners mention of Martial Arts in China brings to mind the film *Hidden Dragon Crouching Tiger* or perhaps if they are much older they remember Bruce Lee with his breathtaking acrobatics. There is much more to the Martial Arts in China than these though.

The Beginning

Confronted with a harsh environment, the ancient ancestors of today's Chinese created methods of attack and protection including gymnastics, jumping and kicking. They already knew how to fight with simple weapons fashioned from wood and stone however it was essential to be able to fight with fists, bare hands and feet.

Kung fu began in the Shang dynasty (1600-1046 BC) and the Zhou dynasty (1046-221 BC). Wrestling followed these skills, sword and spear skills added during the Qin dynasty (221-207 BC) and the Han dynasty (206 BC-220 AD). Further developments occurred during the Song Dynasty with different schools of the martial arts forming. Some specializing in the hand to hand combat while others were mainly about the skills of weaponry.

Development

Chinese Kung Fu, commonly called Wushu or Gongfu, consists of a number of styles of fighting developed over the centuries in China. Today it is becoming increasingly popular throughout the world. Some see it as a symbol of Chinese culture and all that means.

Some of the styles such as Shaolin, Qigong and Tai Chi are very well known and are now practiced throughout the world by millions and millions of Chinese and non-Chinese people. Some foolish people, particularly in the West, think all Chinese people have mastered Kung Fu. Obviously, this is nonsense but the sport is definitely associated with China.

Despite it being a fighting style Kung Fu stresses peace and honor. Definitely not violence; definitely not aggression. Generations of exponents of kung fu have upheld this idea. Kung Fu was originally designed purely for self-defense but now it's practice is seen as a very useful way of promoting physical fitness.

Classification

Over many centuries Kung Fu has developed into a huge system with a large number of schools. They are more than 300 types of it in China alone. The style in northern China is quite different than it is in southern China. Some schools are named after their location. An example is the Shaolin, which is from Shaolin in the province of Henan.

Shaolin temple is the ancestral temple of the Chan or Zen sect of Chinese Buddhism. It is located on Mount Songshan in Dengfeng county, Henan province.

The Shaolin Temple gradually developed its own cultural system. The system embraces Chan (which means sitting in meditation), wushu, medicine, ancient architecture, historical literature and books, as well as food and drink, and daily life. In other words a complete way of life.

The most important parts of Shaolin culture are:

(i) Integration of Chan meditation and wushu, with wushu embodying Chan;

(ii) Medicine as supporting wings of wushu

(iii) and the good things of other schools.

There are two prevalent but contrasting beliefs regarding the origins of Shaolin gongfu:

(i) it was created by Dharma;

(ii), Huiguang and Zeng Chou, disciples of Batuo, the founder of the Shaolin Temple, created it.

2. Wudang Martial Arts: Mount Wudang is considered one of the sacred birthplaces of Chinese Daoism, also being the cradle of legendary Wudang quan--a kind of gongfu that pays more attention to the inner work and strength. It is also famous for its incomparable scenery and described as the No. I "Mountain of Immortals" in the world.

Since ancient times, Daoism has advocated practicing the Dao (Way) with indifference to fame and fortune, with restraint in behavior, and boxing to be practiced only by its disciples. This was a major obstacle to any widespread promotion of Wudang gongfu. Moreover, Daoist wushu was also limited by its religious discipline of what is called "speaking of the founder rather than the masters." This has made it difficult for others to study it in any depth if they object to religion.

Wudang quan derived its name from Wudang Mountain. It is one of the major schools of Chinese martial arts. In the wushu world, there is a saying: "Shaolin is respected in the north and Wudang in the south," its characteristics include: checking motion with stillness, overcoming the strong with the soft, subduing the long with the short, stopping the swift with the slow, directing the Qi (energy) with the will, and motivating the body with Qi.

Chivalry

Like most old countries China has a tradition of honor and chivalry. China had a deep culture of reclusion and reflection in ancient times. Outstanding men who had attained a deep comprehension of worldly affairs frequently chose to live alone as hermits and be independent in the latter part of their lives, rather than to endure the hurly-burly of everyday life.

As Chen Wangting, the founder of Chen-style Taiji quan, advised: "Practice Taiji quan in leisure time, and do farm work in the busy season." With this attitude of total dedication, the genuinely chivalrous swordsmen and wushu masters often retreated to obscure places. Wushu was the tool they used to meet the needs of their cultural life.

Wushu masters had the highest standards, which saw them value justice, ready to help others at the risk of their own lives, cherish brotherhood and personal loyalty, and never break a promise.

The motto was, "The most important thing for a chivalrous swordsman is to serve the nation and the people." The great integrity of chivalrous swordsmen was what most ordinary people did not have but aspired to. Wushu was such that the path to the spiritual realm of the chivalrous swordsmen was gongfu.

Heroic Novels of Chivalry

Ever since antiquity, China has had heroic novels. Counted among the best-known novels are: *Outlaws of the Marsh*, *Tales of Chivalrous Swordsmen*, and *Stories of Young Heroes and Heroines*. *Outlaws of the Marsh* became an eternal Chinese classic.

In modem times, 600 to 700 published novels of chivalry have been recorded. The contemporary novels written by Jin Yong, Liang Yusheng, and Tau Long are very popular in the Chinese world.

The value of these heroic novels lies in the fact that a fictitious world is carefully and cleverly woven by the authors, who have made use of the extraordinary military skills of gallant chivalrous swordsmen and swordswomen to depict the power of idealism, it frequently carries moral messages in a subtle yet adventurous way.

The root cause of the Chinese chivalrous complex is the longing for the realization of personal worth in life, along with an absolute abhorrence with all the innermost heart to social injustice. Novels of chivalry can be regarded as "fairytales for adults."

How it started

In times gone by people used a very clever hunting device called "rope to trip beasts." It consisted of a long rope with one end tied securely to a stone ball. The hunter, with the other end tied around his arm, would chase a wild animal and cast the stone ball towards the animal as he approached it. The stone would pull at the rope and tightly wind it around the animal's leg, thus trapping the animal. This ancient rope was the embryonic form of the wushu lasso weapons used by t later generations.

Traditional wushu weapons such as "meteor hammer," "flying talon" and "flying hammer" all originated from it. Due to unceasing development through primitive wars, the productive instruments that had been used for hunting gradually became refined into various weapons for the purposes of fighting and killing people.

Primitive military drills were gradually started in the form of "field hunting" and "armed dancing." "Field hunting" meant the training of soldiers to use various weapons and tactics, as well as to lead horses and chariots. "Armed dancing" referred to fighting between humans and wild animals, and between men and men, an imitation of hunting and battle scenes. The application of the experience of combat and killing in war to routine training was, in essence, the embryonic form of Chinese wushu. That is how it started.

Swords

The manufacture of swords through the process of smelting has been done for over 3,000 years in China. The sword was a symbol of power as well as a protective weapon for rulers when it first made its appearance. As smelting technique improved, the swords were not only much more destructive to the human body, but also easier to carry, and so were widely used in wars.

About 2.200 years ago, ancient Chinese craftsmen were able to make high-quality bronze swords. At the same time, swordsmen and professional warriors also arose among the people. In ancient China, when swordsmen and swordswomen were learning to use swords, they often encouraged themselves to harder study with the saying, "It takes 10 years to learn the skills of sword use."

Women

Women began to practice martial skills during a unique period through the years 220 -589AD. Especially among matrilineal clan nationalities, women held high positions. When they came to the Central Plains for trade, they displayed their indomitable martial spirit. Some women of noble families mastered superb martial skills and even commanded troops to fight battles.

Official Examinations

Wu Zetian, the first empress in Chinese history, in 702 AD. began to adopt a system of imperial examinations, specializing in military skills, as a way to select military personnel. This greatly promoted the popularization and improvement of the martial skills of military personnel and civilians.

The examination consisted of three parts: 1. Military skills: mainly archery and spear skills; 2. Strength and endurance: namely weightlifting and load carrying 3. Bodybuilding and conversation skills. As it was more scientific and standardized than any previous method for selecting military personnel her system continued to remain in use for more than 1,000 years until it was abolished in 1905.

Chinese Wushu and Japanese Judo

Wushu routine techniques were greatly developed during the Song Dynasty (960-1279), mainly to meet demand for civilian entertainment as well as in military training. More attention began to be paid to bodywork, physical strength, rhythm and movement design.

Each routine consisted of a starting position and a finishing position. Before a routine began, the trainee had to make a fist holding salutation as a sign of courtesy. This was an important symbol of maturity in the development of Chinese wushu.

Associations for practicing wushu were very popular among the common people in the Song Dynasty. The formation of associations created favorable conditions for the teaching, exchange, and development of wushu among the people. Moreover, there were organized, regulated, open wushu competitions with prizes, which had been rarely seen before.

The thrilling description of how Yan Qing, a hero in Outlaws of the Marsh, dashed at his opponent using a stratagem on the stage, in the 74th chapter of the Chinese classic, is a vivid commentary on the popularity of wrestling in the Song Dynasty.

Japanese karate, judo, and Chinese wushu are closely related in their origins. The book *Quan Jing* (Chinese Wushu Classic), written by Ming Dynasty (1368-1644) grand general Qi Jiguang was available in Japan around 1600.

A Chinese martial expert of that time, Chen Tuanyun went in 1619 to Japan where he taught Chinese wushu. Three of the students he taught created ancient Japanese jujitsu, (later renamed 'judo') after learning Chinese martial arts. These three students were considered by later generations to be the founders of Japanese judo. So it was that Chen Yuanyun contributed to the founding of judo in Japan.

Armed Guards

When we read a Chinese novel of chivalry or watch a kung fu film, we often come across agencies providing armed escorts and bodyguards. This phenomenon started in the late 17th century. Such agencies arose, grew and died out during the Qing Dynasty (1611-1911), through a history of more than 200 years providing some interesting pages in the history of Chinese martial arts.

These agencies not only provided economic opportunity in the society but also provided a livelihood and the chance to earn money through genuine skills for the wushu masters. Wushu gave the basic expertise on which the agency depended for its survival, and the armed escorts employed by the agency had to be wushu masters with special skills, otherwise they could not do the job.

Among the different schools of wushu closely related with the armed escort agencies, Xingyi quan was the most influential school, and became most closely connected with the armed escort agencies. A Chinese wushu proverb says, "Taiji quan will not injure people after you practice it for 10 years while Xingyi quan will kill people if you master it in one year." This demonstrates the tremendous combat force of Xingyi quan.

Yin and Yan

The *Book of Changes* says, "There is taiji in the changes which is divided into two polarities." The two polarities are exactly Yin and Yang. The name of 'Taiji quan" (shadow boxing, or Tai Chi Chuan) is precisely based on the theory that the taiji (the Supreme Ultimate) is divided into Yin and Yang, and Yin and Yang are integrated into the taiji.

Wu Shu says in his book *Records of Arms*, "Attack is Yang, and defense is Yin." In *Theory of Taiji* Quan, Wang Zongyue wrote: "You should know about Yin and Yang: adhering means moving away and moving away means adhering; Yin is not separated from Yang, and Yang is not separated from Yin.

Only when Yin and Yang are put together, can you acquire the knowledge of strength." In *Illustrations of Chen-style Taiji quan*, Chen Xin said "The key to Taiji quan lies in the two words: 'opening' and 'closing.' The wonderful thing about Yin and Yang as boxing lies in the way in which each is the root of the other."

The Theory of Five Elements

The theory of the five elements has been prevalent since before the Qin Dynasty (221-206 BC). It became part of many aspects of the daily life of Chinese people. The theories of many types of quan or boxing in Chinese wushu involve the theory of the five elements.

Five-element boxing in Xingyi quan is directly derived from the principle of each producing and being overcome by the other, in the theory of the five elements. Taiji quan also defines its five basic foot techniques as the five elements: "step in (fire), step back (water), step to the left (wood), step to the right (metal), and keep to the central position (earth)."

The development of wushu has a close bearing on Chinese medicine. The Yin and Yang theory of the five elements permeates all aspects of the theoretical system of Chinese medicine. The Yin and Yang theory of Chinese medicine deals with relations of opposition and restraint, serving as each other's root and using each other, growing and declining while balancing and mutually transforming into each other between the functions of the human body and the natural foundation.

The five elements theory of Chinese medicine exposes the functional structure of mutual growth and progressive mutual restraint between the major internal organs and tissues inside the human body, and between the major factors of the internal and external environments of the human body.

The theory of Chinese medicine regards the heart, liver, spleen, lung and kidney as the five internal organs, drawing an analogy between them and the five elements, i, e. heart as fire, liver as wood, spleen as earth, lungs as metal, and kidneys as water. As the five elements each produce and are overcome by the others in a certain order, the five internal organs have the same relationships.

Therefore, pathological changes in some internal organs in the human body often lead to the functional imbalance of other parts. The relationships between five-element boxing and the five internal organs of the human body: 'outward punch" improves the liver, "cannon hammer" improves the heart, "horizontal punch" improves the spleen, "straight arm chop' improves the lungs and "drill chop" improves the kidneys.

Chen Wangling of the Ming Dynasty wrote in his book *Quan Jing* (Boxing Classic); "The five internal organs are the source and root of life. They are the heart, liver, spleen, lung and kidney. The heart belongs to fire, which gives rise to inflammation; the liver belongs to wood, which is either straight or bent in form; the spleen belongs to earth, which has a great momentum; the lung belongs to metal, which can be transformed into other things; the kidney belongs to water, which has the function of moistening other things..."

The functions of the five internal organs, solely motivated by the vital energy (Qi), all cooperate with each other. All those who teach wushu cannot get away from this." We can thus see from this, the important place of the theory of the five elements in Taiji quan.

Wu De (Martial Virtues)

As an important military skill in ancient times, wushu required soldiers to be brave and stalwart. Though it is no longer prominent as a military skill today, martial arts are still considered to have great importance in the cultivation of fine moral character, through striving unceasingly to be stronger and enduring hardships.

In wushu, both performers and spectators demonstrate their fearless spirit by going forward bravely. Even Taiji quan, which is performed gently and slowly, also stresses the spirit of vigor and promise.

On the relationship between hard work and success it has been said: "If you want to be above ordinary people, you must be ready at all times to take arduous and tedious training as your greatest pleasure. The more ready you are to accept such torment the more possible it is to achieve success beyond your dreams."

The process of working diligently is, in fact, a process of self-emancipation, of freeing yourself. By the tempering of the body and the mind you will gradually and inevitably release yourself from the yoke of techniques in terms of your body and from the shackles of knowledge in terms of your mind, so that there will exist no more obstacles between the body and the mind, with the body and the mind becoming integrated as one.

Superb skill enables the body to freely convey your innermost thoughts and wishes.

Chapter 5:
Old World Medicine In Ancient China

Yin and Yang

Here are some Yin things: female, Earth, night, moist, cold, small, chronic. Here are the corresponding Yang things: male, Heaven, day, dry, hot, large, acute.

These are quite mysterious to the Western mind but are a very important part of traditional Chinese philosophy. Everything we know of is either Yin or Yang. For thousands of years, the idea of changes between Yin and Yang has exerted a deep influence on the feelings Chinese people about their daily lives and the world. Nothing is all Yin or all Yang, everything has some of each with a balance that is always in change. Yin and Yang are complementary despite being opposites. As they turn into each other they are not independent of one and other.

The Yin and Yang theory of Chinese medicine sees these relationships as push and pull, they are each other's foundation and they use each other, to expand then retract, all the while keeping a balance and mutually changing one into the other through the functions of the body and the foundation provided by nature.

The theory of Chinese medicine classifies body parts using these concepts and something called the 5 phases, a method used in many different systems and situations. It is a method used to explain a wide variety of things including the interaction of body organs. The 5 Phases are Wood, Earth, Water, Fire and Metal.

This method of describing interactions was fully developed by the second century BC. During the Han dynasty. A concept that many readers will be familiar with is that of Feng Shui, which is a method of determining whether a home will have good 'vibes'.

Traditional Chinese medicine believes that there are passages in the human body through which vital energy (Qi) circulates to regulate bodily functions and tributaries that branch out from the main passages. Along the main passages and tributaries are distributed the meeting points of the passages of blood and Qi, which are known as the acupuncture points. The passages and their tributaries are known as meridians.

The practice of acupuncture is based on Yin and Yang. Acupuncture involves the insertion of thin needles into the body. It is a practice, which is usually quite safe if a person who has been trained properly does it. As well as veterinarians on animals can use being a method of treatment for humans it.

In traditional acupuncture, the acupuncturist makes a decision as to which points the needles are to be inserted by a close examination using acupuncture theory. Among the body parts and functions checked are tongue, body odor, body temperature, breathing, appetite, elimination etc.

There is more to Chinese medicine than acupuncture. Other things are massage, herbal medicine, exercise and nutritional therapy.

Massage

The practitioners of traditional Chinese medicine believed that Qi in the body has to flow without interruption in order for help an individual to be free of stress and free of diseases. Chinese massage has techniques called the 'Tui na' and the 'Zhi Ya.' The techniques are different, but both are very effective. It is necessary for a minimum of 30 minutes of either type of massage regularly.

There is a close relationship between acupuncture and Chinese massage. Both focus on acupuncture points that when stimulated assist the transportation of Qi through the body via the meridians. The aim of doing this is to achieve a balance of Yin and Yang in order to prevent different infections and maintain all organs in prime condition.

If the meridians (channels) are obstructed or impeded, the likelihood of health problems is greatly increased. Properly trained massage therapists can diagnose which meridians are blocked and which acupuncture points require pressure. It has been shown that regular massages of this type are very beneficial for severe pain in the back, problems with the cardiovascular system and sufferers of arthritis.

The massage type called Tui na involves the stretching, squeezing and moving the muscles. The other type, Zhi Ya, presses and pinches acupressure points with the same aim. Both techniques stimulate the body so that it releases hormones, regulates the flow of blood, boosts energy and assists recovery from pain and injury. The idea is to achieve the best balance of Yin and Yang in order that full health will be achieved.

Chinese massage therapy has for a long time provided pain relief for muscles that are sore and injured. Chinese massage therapy improves the flow of blood to areas, which have been injured or are sore from exercise, and helps get rid of the buildup of lactic acid that causes soreness after exertion. Chinese massage therapy helps in gaining and maintaining a mood, which is calm and relaxed. Regular massage boosts the immune system and stops the body developing illness in the internal organs, muscles, and bones.

Herbal Medicine

Chinese herbs have been used for medicinal purposes for many centuries, perhaps as early as 2800 BC. A book from about 100 B.C. during the Han dynasty lists 365 items, which include roots, grass and other things that are used in treating ailments.

A book which appeared later in the Han dynasty employed Yin and Yang and the 5 Phases in its descriptions of herbal treatments. There were developments and additions to the therapies in the book as the centuries passed. This book and others have herbs and their use listed but also talks about therapies involving human and animal parts as well as other ingredients. There is a lot of mixing involved in preparing these herbal medicines. Ideally, a patient will have a special mixture tailored for he or her.

The medicines are classified by a number of methods. The first is *Four Natures*. The natures are hot, warm, cold and neutral. Obviously, they relate to temperature.

The second is *Five Flavors*, which are acrid/pungent, sweet, sour and salty. The reader may wonder about the terms acrid/pungent, bitter and sour. In English, they all mean the same however in this situation they refer to the degree of bitterness.

The third method of classification is *Meridians*. This name refers to the meridian and organ concerned.

The final method of classification is *Functions*. This refers to the action that the remedy is to cause such as vomiting or expelling woodworms.

Exercise

Traditional Chinese medicine looks at the person in his or her entirety. Each person is a whole being with body, mind, and spirit interconnected and supported by an underlying energy system. There is a very strong interconnection of the spirit, mind, and body with Qi. As a consequence, the way in which exercise should be done for best health is very important.

Too much sweat is not beneficial and can cause serious loss of Qi. Traditional Chinese medicine views exercise, which produces a lot of sweat as being harmful to the heart. Exercise, which overworks the tendons and ligaments, reduces Qi of the liver. It is the liver that has to produce more energy when these are taxed. This is viewed as a particularly serious problem for women.

Traditional Chinese Medicine has always seen exercise as having a vital role to play in the attainment and maintenance of good health but is opposed to heavy exercise such as long distance running. Traditional Chinese Medicine promotes exercise regimes like Tai Chi and Shaolin which approach exercise in a way that caters for all the myriad interconnections referred to before and incorporates meditation.

Western science has repeatedly demonstrated the positive effects of meditation such as improving the immune function, lowering blood pressure and most importantly reducing stress. The exercise systems endorsed by Traditional Chinese Medicine such as Tai Chi and Shaolin emphasize slow, peaceful movements, which assist the flow of Qi throughout the body. When this is done health is promoted and life prolonged.

There is a chapter in this book on Chinese Martial Arts or wushu as they are called in Chinese. Although the practitioners of this activity train with great effort and discipline the ideas about exercise are completely embraced in wushu.

The fundamental concept in Chinese Philosophy is harmony between humans and nature. This is founded on the idea that humans are part of nature, and the paramount ideal of life is the deliberate attainment of harmonious integration with nature.

This idea of a perfect harmony between humans and nature is encapsulated in wushu. Its exponents, who using wushu are making themselves at one with nature, show it.

In other words, the practitioners of wushu are very serious about achieving harmony with the natural world. The natural world includes adjustments for the climate, the geographical position, the seasons, and even the compass direction.

They use different methods and materials; suitable for the particular location and time they are practicing in. They tend to choose places, which are quiet and beautiful for their practices.

The desire for total harmony between nature and humans put an emphasis on the following of nature as the guide while wushu was being designed. As an example, there are types of wushu named after animals, astronomical phenomena and plants such as 'tiger and crane,' 'eagle-claw' etc

Nutritional Therapy

Traditional Chinese Medicine food or nutritional therapy was first written about, in 650 A.D, by Sun Simiao, during the Tang Dynasty. The thrust of the book was a preference for people to use food rather than drugs when they were sick. In the book, there are 154 descriptions of the properties of different foods in terms of Qi and the 5 Phases. Sun Simiao had a disciple called Meng Shen who wrote a book on the therapeutic worth of diet. No copies of this book remain now but it is described in other texts.

In these books, foods were described as 'heating' foods such as meats and ideal for conditions like anemia and fatigue. Other foods were described as 'cooling' and included green vegetables. These foods were described as being ideal for conditions like rash and constipation.

It is significant that if we judge these pieces of advice written so long ago by the yardstick of today's research that there is nothing to contradict this advice. It has been verified.

Those who emphasize diets of raw foods, such as some vegans, are giving incorrect advice according to Traditional Chinese Medicine.

(1) no single dietary rule is correct for everyone. Each person needs a unique diet.

(2) raw foods tend to be cold foods and if overeaten there is the risk of damage to the spleen.

(3) the feces of people on this diet could be loose if they eat too many raw vegetables. This is a sign of spleen damage according to Traditional Chinese Medicine.

A diet that has received a lot of publicity and official praise is the ketogenic diet. These diets were used in the in the 1920s and 1930s and proved effective in the treatment of epilepsy, however, they fell from favor as other treatments became available. A crude description of a ketogenic diet is that it is a diet high in fat, sufficient in protein, and low in carbohydrates.

An analysis of this diet can be made using the paradigm of Yin and Yang and the benefits can be explained. Once again though the message from Traditional Chinese Medicine needs to be heeded and that no single dietary rule is correct for everyone. Each person needs a unique diet.

Before finishing this chapter on Traditional Chinese Medicine we will examine its use of a number of foods that have had a lot of favorable publicity in recent years.

Turmeric

Turmeric is an herb from a plant with that same name. Turmeric is perennial; this means that it has a life of two years or more. The plant is a member of the group of ginger plants. It comes from India.

It came to China as a result of trade with India. Marco Polo told about it being used in China in the notes he wrote about his 13th-century visit. Turmeric has successfully been used with many diseases of the stomach, the circulatory system, and arthritis. Turmeric is an antioxidant and it is anti-inflammatory.

Although practitioners of Traditional Chinese Medicine were unaware of this terminology, which was unknown then they were certainly aware of the powerful properties of turmeric.

Coconut

Coconuts are the large brown fruit that grows on coconut trees. Coconuts are found in warm climates. In China, coconuts grow throughout the southern part near the coast. Using the food classifications we introduced earlier from Traditional Chinese Medicine they are 'warming', they are 'sweet', they help the body produce fluids, they assist urination, and they expel worms

Cinnamon

Cinnamon is a well-known herb with a very distinctive smell. Most cinnamon in shops is the Sri Lankan variety but this is not the variety used in China. The other types of cinnamon have stronger aromas and are the *Cinnamomum cassia* tree from the Far East and the *Cinnamomum loureirii* tree from Indonesia.

The type used very widely in Traditional Chinese Medicine (TCM) is cassia. In TCM cassia and its derivatives are called Gui Zhi. In the texts, it is described as being of benefit in fighting colds and flu (the texts refer to them using different language), arthritis, erratic heartbeat, breathlessness, diarrhea, and flatulence. Clearly, the practitioners of TCM were onto a winner here.

Oregano

Oregano is another well-known herb. It is native to Northern Europe and Asia. It has been known in China for centuries and has been used by TCM for vomiting, dysentery, fever, colds, jaundice and diarrhea. Very similar to cinnamon although not as widely used.

History

Exercise

This probably began about 2000 BC. During this time the martial arts took relevant parts to start wushu. During this time wushu was concerned only with fists, bare-hands, and feet.

Massage

Probably this therapy started very early.

Herbal Medicine

There are indications this started as early as 2800 BC.

The Han Dynasty

Acupuncture

Acupuncture is mentioned in a book on medicine that was published about 100 BC. Some experts believe that it had an earlier start than that, though. Its popularity in China was dependent on the dynasty that was in power at the particular time. Its popularity rose and fell accordingly.

Massage

The practice became more formalized.

Exercise

During this time wrestling and weaponry became part of martial arts.

Herbal Medicine
There were two books published. The second shows the increasing formalization of herbal medicine.

<u>Tang Dynasty Onwards</u>

Exercise
During this time the Okinawans who passed it on to the Japanese who used it to create karate adopted kung fu. Also during this time, a number of new wushu schools began.

Nutrition
The first nutrition therapy books appear

<u>Circa 1100s</u>

Nutrition
Increased trade brings new foods for nutrition therapy.

Herbal Medicine
Increased trade brings new material for herbal medicine.

Traditional Chinese Medicine in the Twenty-First Century
The revolution, which overthrew the Qing Dynasty had some people in China suggesting that TCM is completely replaced by Western Medicine as the people saying this thought that it was better. In the end that was not done and when the Communists came to power in 1949 they introduced a system of barefoot doctors that provided some medical help to the vast number of people in China who had no medical care at all. The barefoot doctors practiced Traditional Chinese Medicine.

Since then there have been many changes, one of the most interesting is the ever-growing interest of the public in the West in TCM. A great disillusionment has occurred in the West, among many people, with Western medicine. Some of these disillusioned people are exploring TCM as a substitute.

Another development is the ever-increasing proof of many remedies in TCM using Western investigatory methods. The ultimate accolade to TCM was when 50% of the 2015 Nobel Prize in Medicine went Youyou Tu whose career has been spent investigating traditional Chinese medicine.

The Chinese spice sweet Wormwood was used 1700 years ago. Tu became the first person to extract the medically active component of the spice, which has the name Artemisinin then explain how it works.

As a consequence of her brilliant work Artemisinin can not only be studied far more easily but also manufactured in very large quantities. This is great news for Third World countries because in these countries malaria is becoming resistant to current drugs.

Mao Ze Dong, the original Communist leader of China, had the idea of making an effective drug for malaria from the plant but decades of work proved fruitless until Tu was successful. Not only is artemisinin successful against malaria but other research is showing that it may be useful against some forms of cancer.

One of the Nobel Prize panelists who selected Tu said that there are many places that open minded scientists get their ideas to develop new drugs. One of the most promising is the huge trove of traditional remedies. It is totally wrong to deliberately ignore this long history of medicines from the past.

As he pointed out, such sources may inspire people to do research on them, but the remedies from the past which were found there need to be updated and thoroughly examined. Never trivialize the very clever means that Tu needed in order to extract the important Artemisinin chemical from its host tree, he said as he concluded.

There are hundreds, probably thousands of old remedies, which are in the archives in China alone. Around the world, there are almost certainly many more and they must be checked.

Another point, which this chapter raises, is the TCM view of beneficial exercise. Although an athlete preparing for an Olympic marathon will need his or her training as it currently stands the value of running for those who only wish to be healthy needs to be carefully evaluated. It may be that the wushu approach might yield far more satisfying results for such people.

Throughout the world the sight of Chinese people doing Tai Chi in parks may just be the tip of the iceberg once others realize the health benefits of this.

Chapter 6:
Military In Ancient China

China has always needed the military in one form or another. Ancient China was completely surrounded by potential enemies who had to be defended against by a strong military that was also needed for China's expansion. Within China, there was a rivalry between different tribes and races.

China was repeatedly attacked from the North and West by what the Chinese referred to as barbarians. Initially, these people were nothing but a nuisance however later they acquired very effective weapons such as cavalry, armor, chariots and powerful devices with which to besiege cities. Brilliant leaders with very good tactics often led them.

These types of problems were a nightmare for the Chinese. Confronted with new weaponry they followed a path traveled by many societies since and adopted these weapons and tactics themselves.

The brilliant Chinese General Sun Tzu wrote the classic military text, The Art of War, in the 6th century BC during the Zhou dynasty. This book is neatly set out in 13 chapters and within each chapter is a list of important points, brilliantly and succinctly written, about the title of the chapter. This book is the oldest military textbook that exists. It is required reading, even today, in all military schools

Xia Dynasty Armies

The first dynasty was the Xia dynasty that ruled from 2200-1600BC. We know little about the Xia except that there were 16 kings, the last of whom was deposed at the battle of

Mingtiao. The Xia were followed by the Shang and Zhou dynasties. In these early dynasties, long campaigns were not possible. China was not yet an empire and would not become one for hundreds of years. Initially, the armed forces were peasants who had been conscripted armed with simple weapons such as spears, clubs, and bows.

Shang Dynasty Armies

By the time of The Shang Dynasty (1600 BC -1046 BC) the use of chariots enabled the Shangs to defeat the Xia A warrior class was forming as Chinese society developed social classes.

The aristocracy were the charioteers. The chariots were the equivalent of the modern tank. They had a crew of three, archer, warrior and driver. The archer could fire multiple arrows. The warrior used a kind of ax, which had a long handle, and a dagger shaped blade. The chariot, just like the modern tank, could serve as a mobile command center and provided a ferocious phalanx of storm troops.

Most of the army were peasants conscripted by nobles on whose land they worked. The nobles were obeisant to the king; remember China was not yet an empire, which required the nobles to equip the peasants from their land. Such a system of social organization is called *feudalism*.

In those days the sovereign led his army to battle. The Shan king had a force of about 1000 that he was responsible for. His largest army was never more than the size of a modern division, about 14-15000.

In battles, apart from the chariots, the bulk of the army were infantry who used spears, long axes, and shot bows. They defended themselves with shields and helmets of leather or bronze.

Fighting was done in massed formations under the pennant of whichever noble had recruited them. The provisioning of even the limited number of troops then was quite formidable and the beginnings of a military bureaucracy responsible for this started to develop.

One effect of the use of bronze is that a sizable bronze industry involving the mining of copper, tin, and lead, the extraction of these metals then the smelting to produce bronze required considerable planning, organization, and effort. This provided a stimulus for the economy.

Zhou Dynasty Armies

The Shang Dynasty was overthrown by the Zhou Dynasty (1045 BC - 256 BC) as a result of corruption and decadence. When the Zhou overcame the Shang the mandate from heaven, which gives a ruling dynasty its power, became theirs. The Zhou dynasty lasted longer than any other Chinese dynasty. In the Zhou, period iron appeared in China. The ability to obtain it from its ore had been discovered by the Chinese.

Throughout Chinese history, there have been wars both with external enemies and within China itself. In the earlier part of the Zhou dynasty, the kings were truly warrior kings leading the battles to unite China and fighting the barbarians.

Over the next few centuries, the authority of the Zhou declined and the power of lords grew. In 771 BC rebels attacked the Zhou capital, Hao, killing King You and overrunning the Wei valley. Although very weakened the dynasty survived and moved its capital to Luoyang in the East. Sadly continuous warfare reduced the many warring states to a small number of kingdoms fighting one another all along the Wei and Yellow River valleys.

For a while shifting alliances kept a balance of power among them, which stopped any one state from becoming too powerful. In this situation, the Border States were favored since they could expand at the expense of their well armed and organized non-Chinese neighbors. By the late 4th-century, it was clear that either Qin in the West or Chu in the south would be supreme and possibly win the empire.

During this time war became far more sophisticated. There was the use of combined operations involving infantry, cavalry, and archery working in concert. Weapons were made of iron, a much tougher material than bronze

Giant armies were used with hundreds of thousands of soldiers, much larger than in preceding times. The bureaucracy required to feed and service armies, which we noted earlier, became far more complex.

During this period the crossbow was introduced. It is thought the Chinese may have been inspired to use it by what they saw their enemies in Vietnam doing. As is always the case in war any weapon an opponent has will be copied and improved. As well as being a very effective weapon the crossbow was easily produced and it was quite straightforward to teach troops how to use it.

The ax talked about earlier was called the dagger-ax and was now fitted with heads of iron, instead of bronze. This was a fearsome weapon and was very similar to the pike, which was being used in the West. Armor became common. It was provided by a leather jacket covered with bronze plates of about the length of a finger. A helmet of toughened leather was worn on the head.

Swords were quite common but during this period were still made of bronze. In large, massed formations these soldiers would have been very formidable foes.

During this time large navies appeared in order to fight for control of the large rivers. The Chinese built great floating fortresses in order to land on enemy territory. These were a type of landing craft, although one totally different to that used in later wars.

During this period Qin went from strength to strength. All of the states against it were beaten back and in 256BC Qin overthrew the Zhou dynasty, establishing the Qin dynasty. In 246 BC the young prince Zheng came to the throne of Qin and in 230BC his armies began a final ten-year campaign during which all of the remaining rival Chinese states were defeated and incorporated into the new state that was being formed.

Master of the entire Chinese world in 221 BC Zheng pronounced himself the First Emperor and decreed that his descendants would hold that title. The Qin dynasty, only two emperors, was very short lived but two things from it are very noteworthy. Qin Shi Huang's most celebrated feat was the building of the Great Wall of China, still regarded as one of the wonders of the world.

The main external threats to China came from nomadic peoples, such as the Xiongnu, who descended from the North and West and conducted quick raids into China, on horseback, in order to loot and pillage. Once they had wreaked their carnage they fled back to the steppes and were rarely caught by the lumbering Chinese army.

It was thought that a barrier against them would keep them out and earlier Chinese kingdoms had already built some defensive walls during the warring states period. Qin Shi Huang had his labor force link these three substantial walls but also extended them over vast distances to complete a 2400 mile fortification in 214 BC.

The wall is a symbol to the Emperor's callous disregard for human suffering. Tens of thousands of laborers are known to have died during its construction. It was lengthened later until it was 5500 miles long (a bit more than 9000 kilometers). Like the Maginot line the French constructed before the Second World War, it proved incapable of stopping determined invaders and the sacrifice of the workforce was in vain.

The second thing that Qin Shi Huang is well known for is the Terracotta army. There were stories about some amazing soldiers in pits, which proved to be true in 1974 when people digging a well uncovered the Terracotta Army. There were thousands of life-sized ceramic warriors, lined up in formation underneath the ground. Later on in 1976 and 1977, another two pits of these warriors were found.

Nothing had been neglected in the construction. There were at least 6000 of these men. There were archers, foot soldiers, and cavalry who were equipped with real weapons and accompanied by chariots drawn by very splendidly modeled horses four abreast. One of the reasons that we know how the soldiers of that time dressed is because of this Terracotta Army.

When Qin Shi Huang died intrigue brought forth an ineffectual second emperor of the Qin dynasty. A rebellion occurred and in 202 BC a man called Liu Bang of the Han people became emperor and was known as Han Gaozu, the first of the Han emperors.

During the Han dynasty, there was the usual internal strife. The Chinese army invaded both Vietnam and Korea and pushed China's borders much further west. They developed the use of cavalry to a far higher level than ever seen before in China. This expansion put a stop to the raids by the nomads in a far more effective way than the wall. It also allowed the Chinese to trade with peoples further west by use of the Silk Road. This led to increased prosperity.

Unfortunately, the Chinese were now suffering from something called Imperial Over Reach where an empire is so vast that it becomes hard to control. There were rebellions against Chinese rule both within China itself and along its border. In order to do this a professional army, better than any possible opponents was needed.

The Han Dynasty ruled China for more than 400 years, interrupted only briefly by Wang Mang, a usurper, who was soon gone. The era was regarded by the Chinese as a golden one and was the era of life by which other eras have been judged.

Unfortunately, the Han dynasty like all those that preceded and succeeded it came to an end in a period of obscure struggles that might be described as the dark ages of China. There were peasant uprisings and civil wars, which disrupted trade and manufacture and undermined the whole economy.

Luoyang the capital went up in flames. The states that replaced the empire were not centralized but very eager to fight rivals so that the 368 year period down to 581 AD featured a lot of strife.

In 581AD an ambitious general overthrew the Northern Zhou then he went on to conquer the South and reunited China and as Wen Sui was the first Emperor of the Sui dynasty.

A key development is thought to have been the institution of *fubing*, which were territorial forces (a peoples militia force). These fubing would become the backbone of the Sui and Tang armies and attract many comments, none of which has helped to clarify their beginning.

Under the Northern Zhou most fubing were probably infantry rather than the cavalry, Han Chinese rather than non-Han, and volunteers rather than conscripts, having been lured into service with exemptions from taxation and corvee (unpaid labor).

There were numerous exceptions, conscription was by no means abandoned, some fubing may have originated in units previously recruited by local magnates and then incorporated into the army, the enormous number of horses shows that cavalry, both light and heavy, remained crucial, so did the recruitment of non-Han forces, and in the North, as in the South, there is evidence for the growth of military professionalism and a martial culture.

Long-term enrollments, with families or groups of families providing recruits from one generation to the other, is evidence and the growth of an esprit de corps may be inferred from the news that as of the 570-580AD the Twenty-Four Armies began to perform guard duty by rotation near the Imperial Palace, an important feature of the fubing system under the Sui and Tang Dynasties. This would be much like 'Trooping the Color' in modern times.

The 'ideology' or 'ethos' of China for most of its history has been Confucianism. Confucius was a great Chinese philosopher. The philosophy of Confucius emphasized personal and governmental morality. It is very strict on the correctness of social relationships, of justice and of honesty. Confucius was not very keen on the military.

Later dynasties acted on this in a way that made it impossible to properly guard the country let alone an empire.

Under the Song dynasty, the emperors slowly eliminated the military influence from the administration, waiting until officeholders left or died and then replacing them with civilian officials.

It was during the Song dynasty that the official class got the elite characteristics, which were famous in the world outside. Examinations had existed for centuries, enabling the rise of the gifted within the Imperial civil service, however members of the upper-class or via nominees always occupied the great majority of posts.

In the Song dynasty, the examinations were open to more candidates and led on to desirable positions in a service that had been reorganized and had a career structure with the prospect of regular promotion. The prizes and prestige involved led to much competition, and the examinations became major events in the calendar, rigorously conducted so as to prevent cheating or favoritism.

Close study of the Confucian classics created a class of scholar-officials with a common culture and a refined, artistic mind. This intellectual culture became the culture of the dominant class, which had replaced the old aristocracy, taking in even those members who did not take the examinations or were not in the civil service.

This was similar for people in 19th century Britain, drilled in Greek and Latin who left school or University to become civil servants, Indian army officers, colonial officers etc. In its own unique way, Song China produced a civilized ruling class, often described by historians as gentry, scholar-officials or the literati; known in the West as mandarins.

The values of the literati soon permeated Chinese society, and it's distrust of the military led to a general attitude of disdain for soldiering. Fortunately for China the first two Songs were military enough to reunite the country by force.

However as the dynasty proceeded China was losing its military capability. This didn't happen overnight, it was like rust or erosion, a slow but debilitating process, eating away at the ability of China to defend itself. The most serious loss was the cavalry, which could have been so valuable in resisting the horror about to befall it

When finally the Mongols under Kublai Khan attacked China was not prepared. The Mongols were superb horsemen, incredibly proficient in using weapons, including bows and arrows, from horseback. Under Kublai's grandfather Genghis Khan they had conquered large parts of Asia, the Mid-East and Europe.

They should have been prepared but they weren't and the country fell to the Golden Horde. A non-Chinese became Emperor and established a dynasty; the Yuan Dynasty. China would not have to endure such catastrophe again until the nineteenth and twentieth centuries.

Finally, it is essential to talk about the war at sea. In ancient China, the first naval battle we know of happened during the warring states era of 481 - 221 BC. Qin Shi Huang the first emperor of the Qin dynasty was successful in reuniting with South China with naval power.

During the Han dynasty, the Chinese began using rudders and they also designed a new type of ship that was called a *junk*. Large naval battles such as the battle of Red Cliffs demonstrated the advanced naval warfare of the East. In one of these battles, one navy was able to destroy a large fleet of a foe with fire.

As regards traveling by sea to other countries, the Chinese had sent envoys into the Indian Ocean by the second century BC. One of the first Chinese to sail into the Indian Ocean and to reach Sri Lanka and India by ship was the Buddhist monk Faxian in the early fifth century A.D. In 674 AD another Chinese sailor arrived in Arabia after a trip in which he visited 36 countries.

Chinese naval ventures would continue into the Indian Ocean until much later and go as far as Africa. The ships used were huge junks. It is interesting to think what the final outcome might have been if this had persisted and developed further.

The Chinese have some very clever people and they had invented the maritime compass. There is a legend they got to Australia long before Captain Cook. There is another claim to have found Chinese characters, etched on rocks in the Americas, of the Shang dynasty! If that is true then they got there long before Columbus or the Vikings!

If they did get as far as America they may have had the same problems the Vikings did in that they did not have the superiority over the natives in weapons to make the establishment of a Chinese colony in the Americas feasible.

Chapter 7:
The Development of Chinese Literature

The development of Chinese verbal and written literature - all of the aspects surrounding it, including records and educational writing, poetry with lyrical beat, fiction and drama – follows a very exciting path. There are many forms of literature around the world; however, Chinese literature the prominent language in the world, and it has not changed much over the last three thousand years. The flow of literature can be traced back to before the 1,400 BCE.

The written and spoken medium of the Chinese language hasn't changed much over the last 3,000 years. The language has maintained much of the same sound and physical identity. Even the words are pronounced the same, other than the slightest gradual changes over time and the standard differences in dialect throughout the country. Surprisingly, even the conquests extending over large spans of time did not change the language. Instead, the conquering forces were pressed to use the Chinese written and verbal language, because they did not have these mediums in their own cultures, or because translating the Chinese language letters and syllables became too difficult.

Chinese lettering and syllables made it difficult for conquers to successfully change the language of the empire. Translating the context of the Chinese language to a non-Chinese language failed three different times. Because of the impossibilities that changing the language posed, the conquers were forced to use the Chinese language (other than the Mongolians, who fled the area in 1368. Due to this difficulty, the development of China's literature was uninterrupted.

General Characteristics of Chinese Literature

Because of the close proximity and the continuous cultural contacts, the various traditions in Chinese literature have affected those of other countries in Asia. The basic script from the written Chinese language and in some areas, the verbal use of Chinese language became the primary language in the majority of areas, at least until the beginning of the 20th century.

The visual character writing within Chinese speech has made a variety of memorable properties upon Chinese writing the and its circulation:

1. Chinese prose, particularly poetic literature, is written in an attempt to bring visual attractiveness to the person who reads.

2. Since the Chinese language is visually aesthetic, calligraphy provides elevated status in the Chinese culture. It's long been considered fine art for more than 16 centuries. It is so beautiful that it is found hanging in homes next to paintings around the world, including in China.

3. Unfortunately, the writing is so complex, it makes literature a difficult part of education. It is much more difficult to learn to read, and even basic reading skills requires a person to understand and pronounce over a thousand characters, graphs, or symbols.

4. The written Chinese language may have serious disadvantages, but it's long been a major factor in uniting a culture, even in cases where China was occupied by another culture, which was forced to use their written and spoken language.

The graphs in Chinese writing serve a different purpose than standard words recorded in languages that are considered phonetic. The sounds do not dictate a specific sound and they can be pronounced using different mannerisms – which allows them to change through different dialects through the country. Even though there are some differences in the way that various geographical areas pronounce words, the various dialects did not develop into different written languages, and remain the same throughout China, like other languages did over time. While somebody from northern China may not clearly underhand the spoken words of someone from southern China, the written language will remain a constant, making it easy for people from various regions to understand one another.

The way each Chinese graph is pronounced has influenced the way that Chinese literature has developed. The reality that monophonic pronunciation is given in each context can lead to misinterpretation and perplexity as soon as it is spoken without using graphs associated with the context.

Chinese poetry, other than relying upon tonal and rhyme meter for its rhythm, is described by its smallness and quickness. There aren't any stories of either people or abstract assortment and barely any account or illustrative sonnets, which are elongated by the gauges of world writing. Focusing on the lyrical, as has frequently been called attention to, the Chinese writer avoids being exhaustive with detail, checking rather the statures of his euphoria's and motivation or the profundities of sadness and empathy. Usually, conjunctions and pronouns are precluded, and maybe a couple words regularly insinuate exceedingly complex musings or circumstances. This clarifies why scholarly pundits and capable interpreters have diversely deciphered numerous lyrics.

The fine lines of separation among writing style and poems is substantially less distinctly attracted Chinese writing than in other state written works. This is unmistakably echoed in 3 main sorts. Fu, as an example, is considered on the fringe amongst verse and composition, containing components of each of these. It utilizes rhyme and meter and not rarely likewise within the stress and intonation patterns, yet instead, in spite of infrequent voyages into the domain of the graceful, it holds the components of exposition without being fundamentally mundane. This records for the assortment of marks specified to the fu by journalists on Chinese writing— idyllic exposition, rhyme composition, composition ballad, song, and exposition verse.

Another genre having a place with this class is pianwen (which translates as "parallel writing"), portrayed by antithetic development and adjusted tonal examples without the utilization of rhyme; the expression suggests "a group of matched steeds," as is inferred in *pian*.

Notwithstanding the polyphonic impact along these lines created, that estimates, it has regularly been made the means of prose like work and discussion. An alternative type, an unconventional change in this boundary, is known as the baguwen (which translates as the "eight legged essay"). Presently by and large viewed to be contemptible of arrangement as writing, for nearly five centuries it ruled the discipline of Chinese composition as the foremost measuring stick in reviewing competitors in the authority common administration examinations. It misused contradictory development and differentiating tonal examples as far as possible by requiring sets of segments comprising of long passages, one reacting to the next.

Historical Timeline of Chinese Writing

Chinese composition has been occupied into two separate streams, which have been separated for more than a thousand years by a division that is more extensive than others. Established, or scholarly, composition goes for the principles and styles set by antiquated essayists and their recognized devotees of resulting periods, with the Confucian Classics and the earliest scholars as preeminent examples. Whilst the varieties might be somewhat different with individual authors, the dialect is constantly far expelled from their verbal dialects.

Endorsed by officials for the written examinations and noble by customary regard for the social achievements of ancient times, this standard turned into the phonetic device of for all intents and purposes all Chinese exposition journalists. Vernacular exposition (baihua), interestingly, comprises of works in the modern language, the ordinary dialect of the creators. Generally thought to be second rate, the standard was devoutly kept away from for experimental literature pending its receipt by authors and dramatists from the thirteenth century onwards.

The Beginning of Chinese Writing

The most established examples of Chinese composition surviving are engravings on shells and bones of tortoises going back to the latter part of what is considered the Shang Dynasty and the predictions recorded after being performed at the imperial court. These engravings, similar to those etched on the famous bronze vessels dated near the close of the Shang Dynasty, are typically short and true and can't be considered writing. In any case, they are critical in that the more than three thousand characters engraved, which over two thousand have been translated accurately, has turned out to be the immediate predecessor of the current Chinese script.

The Use of Literary Myths

Early Chinese writing doesn't offer, as the literary works of particular civilizations elsewhere does, incredible sagas epitomizing fanciful legend. What data exists is scrappy and incomplete, giving no reasonable confirmation that a natural tradition ever occurred; in the event that it did, the sum of what follows has been lost. Endeavors by researchers, both from the East and the West, to reproduce the legendary tales of times long past have subsequently not progressed past likely propositions. Shang administration material is restricted.

Sources from the Zhou Dynasty are more abundant, yet it must be stressed that they had to have been complemented by Han Dynasty works that, be that as it may, must be perused with incredible alert. It is this, then, the situation we find ourselves in since Han researchers revamped the antiquated writings to such a degree, to the point that nobody is very certain, beside obvious fabrications, what amount was purposely reinterpreted and what amount was altered in compliance with common decency trying to clear up ambiguities or accommodate inconsistencies.

The early condition of mythology from ancient China was additionally shaped by the spiritual circumstances that won in China in any event after the Zhou success (c.11th century BCE), at what time spiritual recognition associated with the clique of the predominant divinities was broadcasted an imperial privilege. In light of his fleeting position, the ruler alone was viewed as fit the bill to offer give up and to go to these divinities.

Shangdi, for instance, one of the major deities of progress and destiny, was distant to people of the peasantry classes. The rulers, the gentry, and the everyday citizens were hence constrained, in dropping request, to venerate lesser divine beings and progenitors. In spite of the fact that this circumstance was enormously changed about the season of Confucius in the initial part of the fifth century BCE, official inactivity and a pattern toward logic blocked the restoration of a fanciful world. Confucius appealed to Tian (Heaven), worried about the considerable penances, however he was not concerned with legends, true or untrue. .

All things considered, amid the last hundreds of years of the Zhou Dynasty, Chinese folklore started to experience a significant change. The old divine beings, all things considered, effectively overlooked, were slowly displaced by a large number of different deities, a number of whom were imported from India with the introduction of Buddhism or were minor deities who had started to be accepted as Taoism sweep throughout the country.

All the while, numerous primary myths were completely re-explained to the degree that a few gods and fanciful considers were excused along with theoretical ideas whilst others were explained as recorded, historical figures. Most importantly, a progressive request, looking like from numerous points of view the institutional request of the realm, was forced upon the universe of the extraordinary. A hefty portion of the bygone myths were misplaced whilst others endured just as parts, and, in actuality, an altogether new legendary world was made.

These new divine beings by and large had obviously characterized capacities and positive individual qualities and got to be distinctly conspicuous in writing and alternate expressions. The legend of the fights among Chiyou ("The Wormy Transgressor") and Huangdi ("The Yellow Emperor"), for instance, turned into a piece of Daoist legend and in the long run gave models to sections of two works of parlance fictional work, known as the Shuihuzhuan and the Journey to the West, also known as the Xiyouji (likewise incompletely interpreted as Monkey). Further legendary figures, for example, the Xiwangmu and Kuafu also gave themes to various ballads and stories.

Recorded personages were likewise ordinarily incorporated with the Chinese pantheon, for Chinese famous creative ability has rushed to bless the life story of a darling saint with amazing and in the end legendary qualities. Qu Yuan, a disastrous official of the kingdom of Chu (771 – 221 BCE), is one of these most outstanding illustrations. Mythmaking subsequently turned into a consistent, living procedure in China. It's additionally right that ancient saints and aspiring legendary figures organized their histories so that it bordered on the mythological by itself.

Chinese Poetry

The principal collection of Chinese verse, recognized as the Shijing ("Classic of Poetry") and comprising of sanctuary, court, and people tunes, was given complete shape some place around the period when Confucius was alive (551 – 479 BCE). Be that as it may, its 305 melodies are accepted as dating between the early Zhou Dynasty and when they were ultimately recorded.

The Shijing is one of the five major Confucian writings, often referred to as the Wujing. The others include the Chunqiu (meaning the Spring and Autumn Annals), the Liji (the Record of Rites), the Shujing (meaning Classical History), and the Yijing (Classical Changes). Since the 2nd century BCE, these five books have been regarded as the highest of all Confucian literature and used in various debates throughout history.

Music would have originally been accompanied to the vocals of these ancient poems, with many of them, particularly religious tunes, were likewise combined with dancing. (In every single ensuing time of Chinese abstract history, new patterns in verse were significantly affected by music.) The majority of these sonnets of the Shijing possess a prevalently expressive patter if the theme is adversity within military administration, love, or regular celebrations, rural errands or country settings, desires or frustrations of the basic people and of the deteriorating nobility classes.

Clearly, the dialect of the sonnets was generally near the day by day discourse of the average folks, and even rehashed endeavors at refinement amid the long procedure of conduction hasn't ruined their brilliance and unexpectedness.

On the off chance that there were ever classic traditions in old China similar to what we find in ancient Greece, Rome or even India, there are few hints of it found within the ancient chronicles. The Shijing possesses a couple of story ballads praising chivalrous actions of the imperial predecessors, however these are organized in sequences, just faintly rough the national stories of different people groups. There is one series, for instance, which records the significant phases the Zhou kingdom went through in their ascent to power, from the otherworldly origins of its ancient creator right through to its victory of the Shang kingdom. These scenes, which, as per customary history, span a time of over a thousand years, and are managed in just around 400 lines. Different phases, that commemorate subsequent military endeavors of the regal Zhou armed forces, are much shorter.

The Shijing applied a significant impact on Chinese verse that, as a rule, has focused on the expressive as opposed to the account component; a reliance upon the final rhymes for melodic impact than on further expository designs; consistent lines, comprising of an average amount of syllables; as well as the use of pitch that is intrinsic in the dialect for beat, rather than the rotation of stressed and unstressed syllables just like the standard in Western verse. The high respect that the collection has been regarded in China derives from its ancient heritage and due to its myth that Confucius, the Great Safe, had altered it. In 136 BCE, the work was regarded as one of the great Confucian works.

In the meantime, another kind of verse, additionally starting in dancing and music, had created in southern China, around the Yangtze River, a zone ruled by the realm of Chu — which ultimately was named Chuci, or "melodies of Chu." These new melodies, which were rich with end rhymes such as the tunes of the Shijing, take after an alternate metrical example: the lines typically appear more and more sporadic and are usually (however not generally) set apart by a solid caesura within the center. Their impact is hence rather mournful, and they loan themselves to droning as opposed to singing. The start of this custom is dark on the grounds that the vast majority of the earliest examples were overshadowed by the splendid fourth/third century BCE works of the excelling prodigy, Qu Yuan, the earliest Chinese poet.

Among somewhere in the range of 25 funeral poems that are ascribed to Qu Yuan, the utmost significant and longest is the Lisao (which translates as "On Encountering Sorrow"). The Lisao has been portrayed as a tribute combining elements of politics and erotica, telling the author's disappointment with his imperial master and how he imagines it would be travelling through far-off lands, describing these accounts in vivid detail as a way of fighting his sorrow. Qu Yuan conferred suicide by jumping into the Miluo River and drowning, his awful demise, not as much as his lovely epitaphs, propagated the new artistic kind. As opposed to the ballads of the Shijing, that would then be followed by a number of successful imitators, the class made by Qu Yuan would be further developed over the next 500 years, as well as experiencing later revivals.

Chinese Prose

Preceding the ascent of the scholars in the sixth century BCE, short composition works were accounted for to be various, yet of these exclusive two accumulations have been conveyed: the Shujing, comprising of differing sorts of the earliest state records, for example, revelations, parts of responsibilities to medieval rulers, and discourses; and then the Yijing, a book on divination. Each of these works were developed by accumulation and, as indicated by an extremely dubious convention, had been edited by Confucius. Both of these can be regarded as literature, however both have applied impact on Chinese journalists for over two thousands years as an effect of them being included within the official Confucian tenet.

The earliest works which are allocated to individual "initiation", is the Laozi, also known as the Daodejing ("Classic of the Way of Power"), long ascribed to Laozi, who is attributed with being the creator of Taoism and the individual who may have been a much older peer of Confucius; and the Analects and the Lunyu ("Conversations"), of Confucius.

Both of these philosophers penned a number of works, and their lessons were documented by their supporters. Hence, the Laozi comprises of brief rundowns of Laozi's idioms, a hefty portion of which are in prose, others rhyme, to encourage remembrance. Similarly, the Analects is made out of accumulations of the sage's sayings, for the most part as responses to certain questions or as a consequence of talks since the materials required were costly and rare. The conditions of the discussions, be that as it may, were normally precluded, and as an outcome the sage's words frequently solid secretive and incoherent, in spite of the significance of the knowledge.

By around 400 BCE, the items needed to produce records and books had improved greatly, and certain changes in writing style came about. The records of the talks turned out to be longer, the story parcels more point by point; jokes, stories, tales, and illustrations, blended in the discussions, were incorporated. In this manner, the Mencius, the lessons of the later philosopher Mencius, not just is much longer than the Analects of Confucius additionally is much more organized when it comes to the subject at hand. A similar trademark might be seen in the bona fide parts of the Zhuangzi, ascribed to the Taoist sage Zhuangzi.

Chapter 8:
Great Historical Figures

Mao Zedong (26th December 1893, Shaoshan, China – 9th September 1976, Beijing, China) and the Cultural Revolution

Also known as Mao Tse-tung and Chairman Mao, Mao Zedong was the most influential figure to emerge in modern Chinese history in addition to the rest of Chinese history. Born in modern day Hunan province, he was a significant Marxist theorist and soldier who led the Chinese people into a communist revolution. From 1935, Mao Zedong took leadership of the Chinese Communist Party (CCP) until the day he died, as well as the chairman of the People's Republic of China between 1949 and 1959, and the leader of the party until he died.

China had been caught up in 50 years of revolution, which Mao settled, and then burst onto the international stage as the most populated country in the world. Mao issued a series of social and economic reforms, taking his place in Chinese history. However, it is true that he didn't take the leading role through the entire event; during the early days of the CCP, Mao was overshadowed by larger figures, although he wasn't an insignificant one and except for during the Cultural Revolution era, most of the decisions made weren't his to make on his own. However, when examining the entire era from the establishment of the CCP until he died, it is clear that Mao Zedong was the main engineer of the new county.

The Early Years

Mao Zedong was born in 1893 on December 26th in a village called Shaoshan in modern day Hunan province. Born to a family, his father had been a peasant previously which had then became rich selling grain and by being a farmer. His education was basic, and his family saw education as a means only to record accounts. He started school in his village at age eight where he learned the *Wujing*, or the Confucian Classics. When he was 13 years old, he had no choice but to begin working on the family farm. He was forced to marry the bride he never wanted – he refused to consummate it and never acknowledged it – and left home, rebelling against his father's authority. He moved to Changsha, the capital of the province. It was here in Changsha where he started learning new notions originating from the west, including those from the Nationalist revolutionary Sun Yat-sen and political activist, Liang Qichao. It wasn't long after he moved here that a revolution started in Wuchang on the 10th October 1911 and within a fortnight, the fighting had transferred to Mao's city.

Mao enlisted in the revolutionary army in Hunan, where he would spend the next six months as a soldier. This limiting time within the military would go on to confirm his admiration for past military leaders and their victories. Some of the great military leaders he had been taught about in school had not only just included the Chinese emperors who led their armies into battle, but also Napoleon and George Washington.

The old imperial period had finally fell in 1911 with the toppling of the Manchus and the following spring saw the start of a new China, the Republic of China. Over the next year, Mao tried out several new things including police school, business school and law school. In secondary school he studied history, reading several classical literary works from the west. Mao's flittering from one thing to another was somewhat similar to the political situation the country itself was experience. In 1905, the official civil service examination system, which had served for centuries, had been abolished and western subjects and methods had begun being taught in modern schools which caused young students to be confused as to continue in the traditional subjects and training or to opt for a modern Western style training, uncertain as to what would be better for the country.

In 1918, Mao Zedong graduated from the First Provincial Normal School located within Changsha. The school, offering secondary levels of education instead of higher education, taught students a range of Western subjects and ideas alongside traditional Chinese philosophy, literature, and history. While he was here, Mao started helping to organize various student societies, giving him his first real taste of politics. One of the most significant of these student societies was the New People's Study Society. Many of those who joined the society, which was established during the winter of 1917 and 1918, would later go on to become part of the Communist Party.

After this school, Mao traveled to Beijing (or Peking, as it was known during the time) where he attended Peking University, which was the most influenceable school in the country. Mao acquired a job as a library assistant for six months, and it was this time that caused a turning point in his life as it was here that he came to be influenced by Chen Duxiu and Li Dazhao, both men who would go on to establish the CCP. As well as this, Mao was at Peking University during the run up to the May Fourth Incident in 1919, which is probably the most crucial event to change the future of the country for the next 50 years.

The May Fourth Incident, or Movement, was a student movement which were protesting against the ruling at the Paris Peace Conference, where it was decided that all the German enterprises and businesses held in Shandong were not to be given back to China, but to the Japanese instead. In addition to this, the name also refers to a period of time starting in 1915, when great changes in Chinese culture, society and politics started occurring. The result was that Leninism and Marxism were starting to replace the Western liberalism in China. We see a transference from the eloquent and mysterious classical language to a more casual and accessible way of writing and speaking at the same time. Younger men started to make their way onto the political stage. While Chen Duxiu may have initiated the May Fourth Incident, it was the students who took the spotlight.

It was from this point, this event, then, that the younger Chinese generation realized that they held responsibility for the future and those who participated would find themselves gaining power in China and Taiwan.

In the summer months of 1919, Mao Zedong would lend his support in the creation of several new student organizations back in Changsha, joining the working people with the merchants, although not with the peasants. Together, they launched demonstrations in order to force the government to stand up to Japan. Many of Mao's writings from this period mention the *army of the red flag*, and by the start of 1921, Mao had finally embraced the notion of Marxism as the philosophical foundation of the Chinese revolution.

Mao Zedong and the CCP

In autumn of 1920, Mao Zedong took the position of headmaster at the Lin Changsha Primary School where he established the foundation of the Socialist Youth League in the area. A few months later, he married Yang Kaihui, who was the daughter of the ethic teacher who previously taught at the school. The following summer, he joined the First Congress of the Chinese Communist Party, which was attended by other supporters from groups all over China as well as from the Moscow branch. Two years later, when the group allied itself with the Nationalist Party (also known as the Kuomintang or Guomindang), Mao Zedong was one of the earliest members to work inside it. With his wife and their two young sons, they lived most of the time in Shanghai in 1924, where he was a principal associate of the Nationalists' Executive Bureau.

During the winter period of 1924 and early 1925, Mao journeyed back to his home village. It was here that he started seeing peasant demonstrations in the area, peasants who had been drawn into political awareness after numerous Chinese had been shot by foreign police in Shanghai. As a result, Mao Zedong suddenly realized that these peasants could play a useful part in the revolution. Even though Mao had been born into a peasant household, his education had developed into the traditional Chinese viewpoint that the peasants were beneath him, dirty and unintelligent. Although he had converted to Marxism, causing him to reevaluate the worth of the urbanized working class, he still held the belief that the peasants were unstructured and foolish as a whole. It was here, then, that he began to see the rural peasantry as the key to turn China around. Taking inspiration from the other members of the Nationalist Party who had begun using the peasantry, Mao started to organize the unstructured peasant demonstrations into a more orderly, structured peasant organization.

The Nationalists and the Communists

It wasn't long before Mao Zedong had no choice but to escape from the military governor of Hunan, and settle in a larger city once more. This time, he fled to Canton, modern-day Guangzhou in Guangdong province, which was the base for the Nationalists. Even though he had escaped to a city, Mao still carried on focusing his efforts on the peasantry and the countryside. He was made the head of the propaganda department within the party, editing the *Political Weekly*. He was present for the second Kuomintang Congress, as well as the Peasant Movement Training Institute, which had been founded in Guangzhou under the watchful eye of the Nationalist party. After Sun Yat-sen had died in 1926, he was replaced as Chiang Kai-shek (also known as Jiang Jieshi), who then removed the majority of the communists from key positions within the Nationalist Party that year. Mao continued working at the Institute until the autumn, with many of the peasants he was training going on to strengthen the communists' positions.

Chiang Kai-shek's Northern Expedition started in July 1926, with him leading his army north in order to attempt to reunify China under his own command, toppling the conventional government and the warlords who had control of the region. Mao went back to Hunan province in November of the same year and in the January and February of 1927, he started inquiring into the movements organized by the peasants, resulting in the belief that it wouldn't be too long before that several million peasants would sweep across the country with no one being able to stop them. However, this wouldn't turn out to be true. The revolution Mao predicted, consisting of millions of peasants, did not occur.

At the same time, Chiang Kai-shek was aiming at forging alliances with the more wealthier classes in both the urban and rural areas, and ignored the working and peasantry classes. In April, he killed the workers in Shanghai who had captured the same city for him. The strategies used by Stalin were not effective for him, the alliances with the Nationalists fell and the CCP were essentially destroyed in both the rural areas and within the cities.

During 1927, in the October, Mao Zedong organized a group of around 200 peasants who had lived through the autumn harvest uprising and started a new kind of combat within the rural areas where the military branch of the CCP, known as the Red Army, instead of the defenseless rabble, would take center stage. However, it should be stressed that the Mao Zedong was able to surround the cities using the countryside as their base to do so, ultimately defeating Chiang Kai-shek and seizing control of China, because of the support of several million peasants. Without the peasantry, Mao would not have been able to do so.

Gaining Power, Slowly

For 22 years, Mao Zedong gained power whilst in the countryside. This period is generally separated into four timeframes: the first is when he and Zhu De, who was the commander in chief of the army, were able to come up with brilliant new strategies using the rural areas as their base of attack. These events, nonetheless, were seen by others, including the Moscow and even the Central Committee in Shanghai, as the interim whilst the next plan of attack was being devised. In 1930, the Central Committee commanded the Red Army to seize control of various key cities in the south-central region of the country in order to influence workers to start a revolution. However, Mao realized that even if they kept trying, the cost would be too great and so he left the battle, refusing to carry out his orders, and returned to Jiangxi. His wide was killed by the Nationalists and so Mao married He Zizhen, a woman he had been co-habiting with since 1928.

The second period is often referred to as the Ziangxi period, which revolves around the foundation of the Chinese Soviet Republic, also known as the Jiangxi Soviet, in November 1931, where Mao became chairman. Support for the revolution was in short supply within the cities and so the guarantee of the overall victory appeared to rest in the slow consolidation and extension of the areas they were based in. At this time, the Red Army had grown to 200,000 men and were able to overpower the army sent by Chiang Kai-shek during the initial four surrounding and massacre attacks. However, the Red Army was still no match for Chiang Kai-shek's elite troops and by the end of the year in 1934, Mao, his pregnant wife, and the Red Army had no choice but to leave the Jiangxi base and make their way to north-west part of the country, which has now been called the Long March.

Historians have been speculating for decades as to how much power Mao truly held at this point, especially between 1932 and 1934, and to which military tactics were devised by him or other members of the party. The general consensus is that Mao was primarily seen as the main figurehead of the party, but wielded a limited degree of power over military and other policies. He attained the de facto leadership in January 1935 at the Zunyi Conference, whilst on the Long March.

Around eight thousand soldiers managed to survive the Long March, finally arriving in Shaanxi Province in the north-west of the country during late 1935. After this, the third part of Mao's rural timeframe commenced, branded as the time when he managed to show a transformed combined front with the Nationalists, working towards ridding China of the Japanese as well as his escalation to unobstructed authority within the party. This time is usually referred to as the Yan'an period, named after the town where they had established themselves), despite the fact that Mao would not settle here until the end of the year in 1936. During the summer of 1935, the communists in Moscow had suggested a united front, and in May 1936, the Chinese communists had suggested the same, this time suggesting that Chiang Kai-shek could possibly join them. In December 1936, Chiang Kai-shek was kidnapped from warlords originating in the north-east of the country, wanting to oppose the Japanese forces and take back the country instead of fighting amongst themselves in a pointless civil war. This kidnapping is commonly referred to as the Xi'an Incident. The Nationalists and the communists had just finished coming to an agreement in regards to a united front, the official agreement proclaimed in September 1937, when the Japanese began making their move to control the country.

Known as the Anti-Japanese War, or the Sino-Japanese War, the communists divided their forces into several smaller units, sending them to the back of the Japanese lines, serving as bases for the rebel forces that basically dominated the rural areas between the urban centers and the methods of communication controlled by the Japanese. Because of this, the Chinese were able to extend their military might up to around a million men by the time Japan surrendered, but it also allowed them to establish political control of a population as high as 90,000,000. Some historians have claimed that the Chinese were able to gain the support of the rural people by using their national pride to stand up to the Japanese; however likely this may be, it is almost certain that agricultural policies would have gained influence and support from the peasant classes.

Between 1936 and 1940, Mao found himself with more time which he could concentrate on leisure activities, such as reading and writing. This period saw him reading translations of various philosophical books by Soviet writers which, in turn, allowed him to create his own works on dialectical materialism as well as producing some of the key works which blended his personal accounts of the revolution and his notions of how it should be continued as they went forward with a united force. In December 1936, Mao produced *Strategic Problems of China's Revolutionary War*, which focused on events and issues within the Jiangxi era; and in 1938, he produced the *On Protracted War*, which tells of the strategies used against the Japanese during the war.

Within his *On the New Stage*, produced in 1938, Mao takes quite a pacifying position with the Nationalists as he tells of the events. He attributes this peace-making attitude as to why they were able to overcome the Japanese and the start of restoration within the country. However, by this time the following year, Mao had taken a different stance, proclaiming leadership by the communist party. Mao declared that the revolution of the Chinese against imperialism – it mattered not whether it was against the Japanese or the British – and so China should be governed by a dictatorship combined of several parties that belonged to the united front against Japan. Mao believed that for this time, the goals of both the communists and the Nationalists were one and the same thing, and as such, the CCP shouldn't hurry to upset the partnership. Yet they shouldn't doubt that they needed to take control of the situation to continue with their socialist plans either. While this was going on, Mao and He Zizhen divorced in 1939 and married an actress known as Lan Ping, who had, at this point, renamed herself as Jiang Qing.

The problems of a Communist and Nationalist competition for the control of the joint front are connected with the continual conflicts for control within the communist party itself. Wang Ming had not long come back to China from an extended stay within Moscow, and Zhang Guotao, who had initially declined to accept Mao as the military and political leadership, both found themselves being blamed of extreme obedience regarding the Nationalist party members. However, more than this, the primary force which caused Mao to emerge as the recognized leader of the CCP is that he understood the need for Marxism to adapt to the Chinese people, their traditions, culture and mindsets.

Mao didn't possess the information that other principal members of the communist party held, including how the philosophy worked in reality, nor could he read the original works by Karl Marx or other writers, something that many of the other members could do. However, Mao declared that he knew and understood China, and the discrepancies between the Russian party and the Chinese soon emerged in 1942 and 1943, during what it known as the Rectification Campaign. This event was created in order to teach a foundation in the theories and principles of the party to the thousands of new members who had arrived since 1937. In addition to this, the other key principal to his rise was what Mao considered foreign dogmatism and getting rid of it.

In the spring of 1943, Mao was able to claim the formal control over the party as he was named chairman of the Political Bureau and the Secretariat. Those not dedicated to Mao or fitted his principals were banished, an operation overseen by Kang Sheng, who would go on later to be one of Mao's most loyal supporters of the Cultural Revolution. Later on, Soviet writers would claim this period to make an effort to expel the

Chinese Communist Party of everything associated or loyal to Moscow. The time running up to the fourth period of Mao's rural time – which saw civil war break out with the Nationalist Party – saw Stalin lose enthusiasm for the Chinese communists being victorious in the country.

The Establishment of the People's Republic of China

Despite Stalin not being encouraging of a Chinese communist victory, both he and Mao had little choice but to deal with the situation when they actually did seize control of the country. Mao declared the establishment of the People's Republic of China on the first October 1949, by December he arrived in Moscow where he arranged a treaty with Stalin which featured a small amount of aid and mutual assistance. Yet, according to Mao's written accounts, Stalin did not begin to trust him until after his support in the Korean War.

Even though there was this undeniable tension between China and Moscow, the earliest policies of the PRC were based on the Russians' own policies. It was soon clear that even though Mao and the rest of the party were able to bring a force of millions of peasants to start a revolution, win using guerrilla tactics and have knowledge of the basic principles of government, none of them had the necessary practical experience required to run a massive economic program, let along an entire country. As a result, the Soviets were the only model they had access to. The Chinese communists began to create a five year plan which was helped with Russian influence which came into effect in 1953, featuring technological help by the Russians and several industrial plants to get them started. However, despite this, it only took two years for Mao to sever the socio-political relationship with the Russians.

The Development of Mao's Path to Socialism

In early 1949, Chairman Mao declared that they would no longer encircle the cities from the countryside, and would, instead, allow the cities to lead the countryside. In 1950, he concurred with Liu Shaoqi over that collectivization, a Soviet policy of organizing all the country's production and industry, when the industries had come up with the right machinery needed. During the summer of 1955, he overturned that decision, stating that the Chinese cultural alteration would be able to continue ahead of the technical alteration. Mao had been awestricken with the accomplishments particular groups had professed to have made despite no external help and so he believed that the Chinese, especially the rural workers, could do it without any assistance. Those who claimed it could not be done he dismissed, calling them old women in front of other members of the party, the same members to whom he bragged about his own achievements and goals. It was soon clear that he made the decisions without the support or even acknowledging the others, and Mao continued to do so.

Before Stalin had been denounced as a criminal by Nikita S. Khrushchev, his successor, Mao Zedong and several other members had discussed a number of ways in order to improve the drive of the intelligentsias so that they could help create a better, more modern, China with the communist party. Mao proclaimed the hundred flowers bloom policy, where the Chinese people had the freedom to offer various thoughts and notions in order to prevent the oppressive regime that had occurred under Stalin within China. Ignoring the advice of his supporters and colleagues, Mao continued with this policy, believing that the conflicts within Chinese culture were mostly unhostile. However, the policy backfired and the people questioned the party, Mao turned on the intellectuals, whom he believed had stabbed him in the back. As a result, those who he felt were not loyal enough were forced to labor in the rural areas, many of whom suffered terribly as they were 're-educated'.

Using this period as his backdrop, Mao would spend the winter period in order to establish the policies which would feature in his Great Leap Forward movement, that commenced in 1958. A technological revolution was still a heavy policy, but continued be wary of any corrupting influences regarding the technical progression and would be sentimental for the seeming transparency and social equality that characterized the socio-politics during the Yan'an period.

In 1958, Mao arranged the peasant classes into what he referred to as people's communes, which would feature in his Great Leap policy. In it, the working rural classes were arranged into units of thousands. However, there was not enough resources to do this, nor was there anyone with the right abilities to oversee it. The consequences were disastrous and the economy suffered greatly.

The winter of the same year and early next year, Mao realized that if he wanted to succeed then he needed to make some changes to his policies. One of these adjustments was the reorganization of the rights to the basic elements of these people's communes as well as downsizing the targets of the industrial and agricultural industries. However, he still continued to promote the basic ideas of these programs, that they could work and were necessary for China as a socialist country. In 1959 at the Central Committee meeting in Lushan, Minister of Defense, Peng Dehuai, condemned the Great Leap policy and its disastrous results. As a result, Peng Dehuai was fired and locked away, eventually dying during the Cultural Revolution. Mao went on to imprison anyone who dared criticize any of his policies, many of whom died during the punishment.

Retreat and Retaliation

Only a couple of members stood up for Peng Dehuai at the meeting, although he had many supporters at the top of the party who remained silent. Lin Biao was made the new minister of defense. Meanwhile, Mao started to establish a new base of power in the People's Liberation Army. Mao started to publicly condemn the new conformist aspects of the middle-classes within the party, both in China and in Russia, as well as the new artistic classes.

The bad blood between Mao and Russia originates in the fact that Khrushchev did not inform him beforehand that the country was going to be de-Stalinized. The Soviet leader also mocked Mao's policies regarding the communes and in 1960, he stopped all technical aid to China, which resulted in several plants in the country being left uncompleted. Russia also tried to pressurize Mao regarding his foreign policies with India and Taiwan – when all of these elements were combined, Mao was angry at the disrespect Russia had shown to him and could not overlook the damage to the economy.

Back in China, Mao had started to worry about the Chinese classes and the economic results of the Great Leap Forward. The Great Leap policy brought nothing but suffering to the people, and combined with several natural disasters, the country was plunged into a country-wide famine where millions of people died. Initially he agreed with Deng Xiaoping and Liu Shaoqi that certain steps were required, but in 1962 he saw these steps as a way of denying the entire concept of the Great Leap Forward.

For the next 3 years, Mao remained in a power struggle regarding the class wars, mainly within the rural areas, and finally in 1964, when confronted by Liu Shaoqi over the class wars, Mao vowed to get rid of the minister.

The Cultural Revolution

Also known as the Great Proletarian Cultural Revolution, the Cultural Revolution has been characterized as one of the bloodiest periods of Chinese history, a time when Chairman Mao tried to radically change the foundation of the party which, as he saw, had been deteriorating for a long time. It was a period which saw the elimination of anyone who stood up to him (as well as those who had ever slighted his wife in the past). Those who suffered from Mao's movement didn't just suffer politically – they were physically beaten and whipped, tortured, force to kill themselves or were murdered. Liu Shaoqi was one of these victims who died since he was refused medical assistance.

The formation of the Red Guards – young Chinese men who were the first wave of Mao's movement – in 1966 saw the country bathed in the blood of its citizens. The Red Guards were a means for Mao to create a stronger, socialist state loyal to him, and they pillaged the country, destroying ancient temples and historic buildings. In early 1967, Yao Wenyuan and Zhang Chunqiao (who would later become the Gang of Four along with Mao's wife), left Shanghai and visited Mao, he proclaimed that the communes were to be dissolved and then replaced with a revolutionary committee.

These new committees were founded on a relationship of those who had once belonged to the party, young campaigners and those who represented the People's Liberation Army. They would remain until two years after Mao died. The committees were initially managed by the army but after the death of Lin Biao, the role of the army had lessened. As a result, it was thought in the early 1970s, that Zhou Enlai could be the one person who could create a more harmonious balance between the old political goals and the underlying principles of the Cultural Revolution.

This balance, however, was upturned even before Zhou Enlai died in early 1976. The Chinese political world was lost in political chaos, with anything remotely foreign considered to be counter-revolutionary. The last ten years of Mao being in power had seen the country praising the First Emperor of China, the man regarded as the most controlling of dictators, and any leader like him, even though Mao had started out with a more democratic view of how the country should be governed.

A Summary

Whilst the Cultural Revolution is often regarded as the most singular important aspect to Mao's revolution, Mao's rule of the country and his place in Chines history should not be judged solely on this time period.

Most historians do not deny Mao's role in how his party devised their guerilla tactics and their overall struggles which would finally see them victorious during the civil war, defeating the Nationalists, as well as the reorganization of lands to the peasantry, and the rebuilding of the country's liberation and dominion. These accomplishments should certainly be weighed against the complete economic and social chaos that spread through China prior to the Cultural Revolution.

After 1949, Mao's reputation becomes uncertain. Chinese historians see Mao acting correctly until mid-1957, when he starts making poor judgements. The Cultural Revolution and the Great Leap Forward policies, the two main policies which would characterize his entire career, were both disastrous and lethal. His ideas were, in hindsight, commendable – having the country rely on itself of others and to encourage patriotism – but the means in which he set about to achieve them resulted in bloodshed, death and humiliation.

When looking at Mao's overall career, it is hard to come up with a conclusion. There is no doubt that Mao achieved vital goals and outcomes for China and her people, establishing changes in the economy, and the re-distribution of the land to the peasantry classes, when balanced against the deaths of millions of citizens who were left starving and those who were murdered during the Cultural Revolution. As such, it could be argued that Mao and his reign, was a fine balance of both good and bad points.

Confucius

Born in 551 BCE in Qufu in the state of Lu, modern day Shandong province, Confucius would grow up and become one of the most influential figures in Chinese and Asian history. Born Kongqiu, he was also known as Zhongni, Kongzi, and Kongfuzi. Confucius is the Romanized version of Kongqiu, and he would be the great philosopher and teacher who would influence politics even thousands of years later, and become deified as the great sage.

The early life of Confucius appears, when compared to his overall importance in history, rather boring and plain. Yet this starkness and simplicity of his life emphasizes that his compassion and benevolence wasn't something that was exposed, but more of a representation of self-development, showing that we as humans can fashion our own destinies. The belief in the abilities of simple humans to transform into brilliant sages and those worthwhile can be founded within the Confucian traditions, and the belief that people can be taught, can be improved and ultimately perfected via individual and social endeavors is classically Confucian.

Facts about the great sage of Chins are in short supply, but what we do know allows us to create a clear timeframe and a general background. For example, Confucius was born during the twenty-second year of Duke Xiang of Lu's reign. For many years, it was believed that he was born on the 27th day of the 8th lunar month but this has been debated about amongst scholars for years and even today, the 28th September in Taiwan is still regarded as his birthday and Teacher's Day.

The sage was born in the state of Lu, or modern day Shandong province, in the town of Qufu. The town and the province overall has long been famous for preserving ancient Zhou traditions, music and rituals. Born Kong Qiu, he later became known as Kongzi, or Master Kong, with the terms Confucian, Confucius or Confucianism derived by the Europeans from the 18th century, and not by the Chinese. However, for the rest of this section, we will continue to refer to him as Confucius.

The ancestors of Confucius' had most likely been of the aristocratic class but had fallen into times of poverty and become commoners before he was born. Confucius' father passed away when he was just three years old. His mother instructed him in various lessons as a young boy but gained a reputation as a great learner during his teenage years. Some of his writings tell of how he had already fallen in love with learning by the time he was 15 years old. When he visited the Grand temple, according to historical records, although he was a gifted student, he felt it was only right that he learn about everything he could whilst there.

Although we do not know who his teachers were, history tells that Confucius had gained various small governmental positions in managing the stables and keeping the accounts for granaries. At 19 years old, he married a woman who was from a similar background to him. He made an effort to study under the right teachers where he learned the six arts – arithmetic calligraphy, charioteering, archery, music and rituals – and when combined with his previous studies in history, poetry and other subjects, Confucius soon found himself in a career in teaching.

He is further accredited as the first person in Chinese history to establish teaching as a job, as well as the first teacher who wished to make education more accessible to the general public. Before the rise of Confucius and his teachings, it was only the upper classes who engaged teachers to teach their sons in certain subjects, and those in government positions would teach the newer members what they needed to know, but Confucius was certainly the first individual to dedicate himself to education as a means of developing and refining society as a whole. It was his belief that everyone would be better off if we continue to develop ourselves. Confucius started a new training course for those who would lead others, welcomed everyone who wanted to learn, and explained that education was not merely amassing knowledge, but improving one's character.

It was Confucius' belief that education was the means by which one could train an exemplary individual, known as *junzi*, a procedure which included persistent development of the self, and continual social contact. Despite the repeated notions of education as a means of improving oneself, true education was essential for public services. He found himself being ridiculed and debated against by hermits who argued his claims about wanting to help the country, and he fought against the urge to live in seclusion, away from the stresses of others humans, and instead, tried to help the country from inside. Confucius would spend years trying to involve himself with the political world, hoping that those who led others would try out his ideas and beliefs from within the government itself.

During his 40s and 50s, Confucius was given the posts of a magistrate and then as the assistant minister of public works, before being finally appointed as Minister of Justice within Lu. It is most probable that he joined King Lu as the chief minister during an official mission. Despite these positions, however, Confucius' political career was brief since he isolated himself from those who held great amounts of power behind the throne. These Ji families, and his strict moral and ethical codes, were not popular with these families who would captivate the king with various vices. When he was 56, Confucius finally saw that his philosophies were not being taken seriously by the king and so he set off to another state where hopefully another king would be interested.

For 12 years, Confucius wandered around outside his home state, followed by an ever-growing band of students. They spread his thoughts, his beliefs and soon enough, his reputation spread far and wide. Confucius knew that he may not be able to achieve what he set out to do, but he attempted to do it anyway. When he was 67 years old, Confucius went back to Lu so that he could teach others and record his beliefs. At 73 years old in 479 BCE, Confucius died with a following of around 3,000 students.

Menicus

Menicus (also known as Mengzi, Meng-tzu, and Meng K'o) was born around 371 BCE in the state of Zhou, located within modern day Shandong province. As with Confucius, Menicus is the European version of his name, and not an original

Chinese name. He was one of the earliest Chinese philosophers who would go on to influence millions over the centuries to his advancement of conventional Confucianism, which saw him being named the Second Sage. One of the most important principals within his philosophy was highlighting the obligation of those ruling to look after the commoners. Within the *Menicus*, it records what the sage told the people and his actions as well as his beliefs of human characters, something that Confucianists have been debating since ancient times.

His Early Life

Menicus' family were from an aristocratic background, settling in the state of Zhou, which was a small state in what is known today as Shandong province. Born sometime around 372 BCE, his early life was very similar to that of Confucius, especially since the states of Zhou and Lu were situated next to each other. Again, like Confucius, Menicus' father died when he was just three years old and his mother focused on the education of her young son. An old story tells of how Menicus and his mother moved house multiple times and eventually stayed close to a school so that Menicus would be brought up in a learned environment, and she went on to encourage him to study well. As a result, Menicus' mother has been praised throughout the centuries as the ideal mother.

While he was a young student, he was taught by a previous student of Zisi, whose grandfather had been Confucius himself. As a result, the traditional Confucian principles were set to be continued. Within due course, Menicus became a teacher, serving as an official for a short time within the state of Qi. Menicus would travel often, granting his wisdom and advice to the different rulers regarding *ren*, which means human-heartedness, where a government was ruled by humanitarian principles. However, this task, no matter how noble it was, was ignored by the ruling classes since they just wanted supreme power.

The time in which Menicus lived, the Zhou Dynasty (1,046 – 256 BCE) was a period when there was a clear distinction and set of obligations between the various upper and lower classes. Over the centuries, those who had coveted power for themselves or their families had risen, with various attempts on control of the kingdoms/states some of which had succeeded, which had deteriorated the foundation of the feudalistic organization and brought about periods of social-political chaos. Because of this repeating pattern, Confucius had been concerned, especially when those patterns had played out several times in a short period. Indeed, the time in which Menicus lived in was referred to by historians as the Warring States era (475 – 221 BCE) when the seven feudalistic states competed with each other for supreme control of the country. As a result, Mencius' pleas on humane treatment to one another were essentially ignored but he carried on with his cause, despite the understanding that it was not a popular one at best.

Theorist for the People

Menicus states that the ruler was responsible for the well-being of those he ruled over. This included the material environments required so they could earn their living, and to provide the ethical and educational direction to improve society. Menicus was able to produce a course in order to achieve economic satisfactoriness for the general public which included smaller taxes, welfare for the elderly and infirm, the almost equal distribution of riches for society, conserving raw materials and resources and free trade. He believed wholeheartedly that when society was stable and enjoyed a stable means of support, could they have a 'steady heart'.

At the same time that Menicus was waiting for the ruling elite to come to their senses and start living a virtuous way of life when it came to their subjects, he would try to remind them that with the Mandate of Heaven came great responsibilities. He declared that it was the people themselves that were the most significant part within a country, followed by grain and the spirits, with the rulers coming last. Within the Classic of History, otherwise known as the Shujing, Mencius states that Heaven sees what the people sees and Heavens hears as the people hear. Because of this, the people saw him as their hero and supported his policies when it came to the central administration.

Menicus traveled to various different states but was unable to find a leader within them who would apply his policies into the way they ran their states. Over the years, Menicus became disheartened with the lack of response and eventually found himself returning back home to the state of Zhou. Back home, he devoted the rest of his time to teaching his students and to record his beliefs and actions with the *Menicus*, which was penned by his students over seven books, one of the earliest historical records of the Second Sage.

Principles of Human Nature

The principles of Mencius' philosophy may be seen as an extension of what Confucius himself had taught a few decades earlier. *Ren* was indeed a concept Confucius taught, the foundation for human nature. However, Menicus taught that the foundation of goodness within humanity, known as *xing*, was the foundation of his philosophy. That everyone was born with *siduan*, or the four beginnings, as realization of the self. When these four beginnings were developed appropriately, they would transform into the aspects of ren which are wisdom, modesty, and uprightness.

Menicus also believed that everyone had the ability to become sages like the old kings, Shun and Yao, who were legendary for their great wisdom and virtues. All people had to do, he argued, was to continue to develop their minds and their hearts. Once they knew both of these, they would know Heaven.

During the Song Dynasty (960 – 1279 CE), Mencius and his philosophy was emphasized by the Neo-Confucianists and even today, the second sage is often seen as the co-founder of Confucianism, with many translations of his works.

Sun Tzu

Sun Tzi is one of the most significant figures from ancient Chinese history. He was born during the Spring and Autumn period (770 – 476 BCE) of the Zhou Dynasty in the state of Qi. This era was a time of great social and political chaos where seven states were fighting amongst themselves to gain control over the entire country. Sun Tzu rose to great heights as a military advisor and general, renowned for his great military strategies, an occupation which was useful to many states at this time when military campaigns and innovations were abound. Before the invasion of Qi, Sun Tzu was able to escape to the state of Wu, where the king offered him a position within his army as a general. Sun Tzu gained a reputation for gaining victories due to his military strategies, soon becoming one of the most important individuals to the state of Wu, and penned his experiences and ideas within a book – The Art of War – which is still read today.

The Life of Sun Tzu

The Art of War is separated into 13 chapters which focuses on a different military subject, discussing various tactics, strategies and fundamental military rules one should abide by. In the Strategy chapter, Sun Tzu debates the concerns regarding why rulers should lead their people into a war. He goes on to describe the relationships between the economy, politics and warfare, and goes on to explain the five basic aspects that require one to think about before waging war on another kingdom or state. The aspects includes the administration of justice system, the generals, what geographical advantages there are, whether there are good prospects and politics surrounding the situation.

Within the Warfare Guidance chapter, Sun Tzu tells the steps required to lead a war, whilst the Offensive Strategy chapter explains how enemies should be fought. He goes on to tell that one must secure a victory with as few causalities as possible; for example, if it is able to be done, avoid bloodshed on the battlefield and subdue the enemy without mass attacks and keep wars as short as one possibly can. Sun Tzu emphasizes that victories at a low price are achievable when the generals and the leader use their skills and cunning. The best way to secure a victory over the enemy is to use political tactics, such as converting one's foe into a useful ally. The next best way of securing a victory is through diplomacy without physical attacks.

The last means of securing a victory is through physical force. Sun Tzu declares that attacking a city is not the best strategy since you need to bear in mind the force of the city in addition to the force of the actual enemy's army. Sun Tzu advocates the use of spies within the enemy's walls well before attacking so that you can get a better understanding of the advantages the enemy has over you. Spies should learn how strong the enemy army is, where it is located, the local geography and to whom the local people are loyal to. When all this information is collected, the generals will be able to produce a successful military plan of attack. In addition to this, counter-spies should be utilized to give wrong information to the enemy's spies.

The Art of War has been copied into various languages and can be found in bookstores all over the world. Many military schools have incorporated the book into their own programs and C.I.A agents are required to read it within their own training schools. The tactics found within *The Art of War* were used during the Battle of Dien Bien Phu during the Vietnam War in 1954 which ultimately saw the French cast out of Indochina, and many other generals have accredited Sun Tzu with their own major military campaigns in recent history.

Laozi

Laozi (also known as Tai Shang Lao-Jun, Lao Dan, Lao Jun, Li Er, and Lao Tzu amongst others), was born around 600 BCE as Li Er and would go on to found the only completely Chinese religion – Taoism. Laozi was the creator of the *Daodejing*, one of the early Taoist texts which is still read today. Contemporary historians are still in debate as to whether this text was penned by a singular author but do accept that Taoism had a great influence on how Buddhism developed within China. Confucianists regard Laozi as a great philosopher; during the Tang Dynasty he was regarded as a royal ancestor, and Chinese people still worship him as a god under the name Lao Jun.

There is no doubt that Laozi remains one of the most important figures in Chinese culture, history and religion, but it is still uncertain as to whether he was a real figure. Most of our information on the ancient sage comes from Sima Qian's *Shiji*, who lived around 100 BCE and the information is not quite as solid as historians would prefer. In it, Sima Qian tells that Laozi was born in the state of Chu (roughly with eastern Henan province) in a village named Quren to a family named Li, and that during the Zhou Dynasty, he held a position known as *shi* in the imperial court. *Shi* translates as historian in today's Chinese language, but back in ancient times it meant a scholar who specialized in divination, astrology and oversaw holy and important texts.

Sima Qian tells of how Laozi journeyed to the west after he realized that the Zhou Dynasty had started to fall into decline. Leaving his home, Laozi made his way to Xiangnu Pass, the gateway to the Qin state. On arrival, he was asked to write a book for Yinxi, the guardian of Xiangnu Pass. Agreeing to the request, Laozi sat down and wrote a book comprised of two parts in which he penned his beliefs regarding the Tao (meaning *the Way*) and the De (meaning *virtue*), which resulted into the Daodejing. Upon its completion, Sima Qian tells that he left and no one ever saw him again.

Sima Qian's account of Laozi then starts to get mixed up with various individuals who have sometimes been identified with. For example, there was a renowned astrologer named Dan, and another being Lao Laizi, who was a Taoist who lived during the time of Confucius. Some ancient writers tell that men such as Laozi could live for an extended period, and it isn't far-fetched to imagine that the Taoists ascribed this notion to the founder of the religion, but it may be a later custom since the fourth century BCE Taoist sage, Zhuangzi, tells of Laozi's death but does not say anything about the sage's long life.

Sima Qian goes on to give information regarding a meeting between Laozi and Confucius but it seems to be heavily mixed up with legends and so comes across as a legend. He does, however, say that the reason why Laozi's life is wrapped in mystery is because the sage preferred a life of isolation. This is something that is seen with many sages and hermits, giving up worldly life for a peaceful life. It isn't improbable to suggest that the author, or the many authors, were most likely those who preferred isolation to reflect on the world.

Scholars are still in debate as to whether Laozi was a historical figure, especially when looking at the *Daodejing*. The book offers various sayings which vary to different dates and some scholars have suggested that Laozi may have, in fact, been a personification of the ideal sage instead of an actual historical person.

Sima Qian

Sima Qian (also known as Ssu-ma Ch'ien) was born in c. 145 BCE in the town of Longmen in Xiayang (modern day Hancheng in Shaanxi province) and would grow up to become the greatest and earliest Chinese historian, as well as a great astronomer. Famous for creating the *Shiji*, which translates as the Historical Records, it is the earliest surviving account of early Chinese history.

Sima Qian was the grandson of Sima Tan, who was himself a great historian at the Han court. At this time, grand historians had many functions which included observing the stars on a daily basis, keeping accounts of events and ceremonies at the imperial court. Before taking a position in the government, Sima Qian traveled widely and went on a military campaign in 111 BCE to southern China. He accompanied Wudi as he made a pilgrimage to Mount Tai, one of the holiest mountains in the country, in 110. In 108 BCE, he was made Grand Historian following the death of his father.

Once in his position, Sima Qian set about a number of new reforms regarding the Chinese calendar. It was also around this time that he started making a record of early Chinese history, a task his father had initially started but never completed. However, before he could finish his records, Sima Qian fell out of favor with the emperor and managed to convince the emperor to castrate him instead of beheading him, in order for him to complete his history. Sima Qian would later find himself rising in favor with the emperor once more but his past experiences had soured him and he found comfort in a quiet life devoted to his works. He finally died around 87 BCE.

Conclusion

Thank you again for downloading this book!

You can email me at adambrownauthor@gmail.com and let me know what you think. I am open to suggestions and will improve this book.

I hope this book was able to help you learn more about China's history.

THANK YOU!

Finally, if you enjoyed this book, would you be kind enough to leave a review for this book on Amazon?

Click here
https://goo.gl/yFRa4X
to leave a review for this book on Amazon!

Thank you and good luck!

Don't Miss this Best-seller on Amazon: 'World History'

Preview here on Amazon for details:

http://bit.ly/ABworldhistory

Made in the USA
San Bernardino, CA
05 March 2017